STARTUP
MONEY
MADE EASY

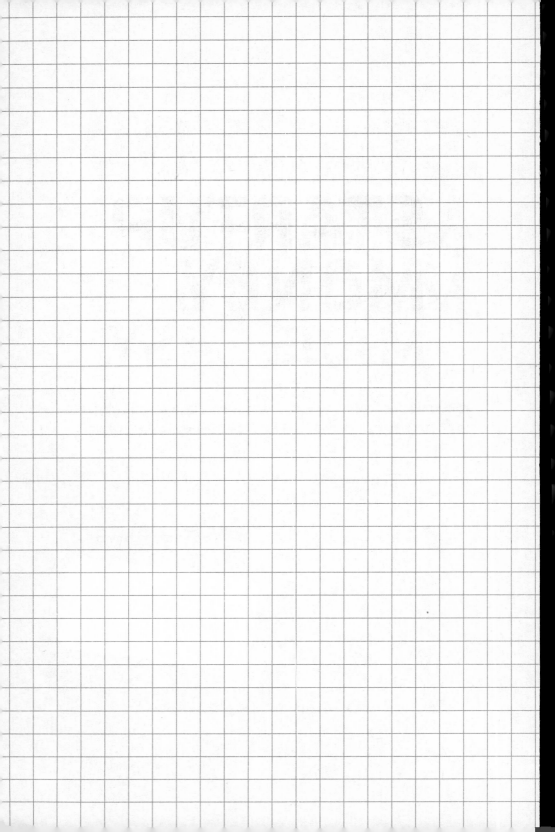

STARTUP
MONEY
MADE EASY

 THE *INC.* GUIDE TO EVERY FINANCIAL QUESTION ABOUT
STARTING, RUNNING, AND GROWING YOUR BUSINESS

Maria Aspan

HarperCollins
Leadership

An Imprint of HarperCollins

Published by HarperCollins Leadership, an imprint of HarperCollins.

Book design by Elyse Strongin, Neuwirth & Associates.

ISBN 978-1-4002-1225-5 (eBook)

Library of Congress Control Number: 2018960959

ISBN 978-1-4002-1224-8

Printed in the United States of America

18 19 20 21 22 LSC 10 9 8 7 6 5 4 3 2 1

>>>> **CONTENTS**

>>>> ACKNOWLEDGMENTS

WHEN WE SET OUT to compile a comprehensive guide to startup money and the financial questions every company founder faces, we found that most of the answers were already at our fingertips.

After all, *Inc.* has spent the past forty years providing advice, education, and inspiration to the leaders of fast-growing private companies.

Our unrivaled editorial content—produced by veteran reporters, all-star editors, and expert columnists—is much of what you see in this book's pages.

A special thanks to former *Inc.* reporter Anna Hensel, who in early 2017 took on an assignment for me and spent several weeks asking countless startup founders to share some of their biggest and most embarrassing financial mistakes—and the wisdom they earned by fixing or recovering from those mistakes. Anna, along with several colleagues who assisted in the reporting, compiled that advice into a fun, occasionally painful, and illuminating feature article I edited, in *Inc.*'s June 2017 issue. "The Smartest Money Advice I Ever Got" directly inspired this book.

Both the article and this book are also indebted to the countless company founders *Inc.* has covered over the years, who have laid bare their financial souls to share their most devastating financial mistakes and the money wisdom they've learned through the years while running their companies. Our thanks to all of them; this book wouldn't be possible without their groundbreaking work.

STARTUP MONEY
MADE EASY

>>>> **INTRODUCTION**

> **"** Ultimately, you know you'll make mistakes.
> The key is trying to minimize the impact,
> and learn from them."[1]

—

VENUS WILLIAMS, tennis star and founder & CEO of EleVen by
Venus

I OFTEN DESCRIBE FINANCE AS the broccoli of running a business. It's good for you, full of nutritional necessities to sustain life—but it's all too often something completely unappealing, overwhelmingly strong, or boiled down to something limp and useless.

During four years spent overseeing the money coverage at *Inc.*, I've tried to turn startup finance into the fun, delicious broccoli—the financial vegetable sautéed with lots of extra-virgin olive oil and red pepper flakes and showers of chopped garlic. The sort of broccoli you might go to a restaurant just to order. The sort of thing you look forward to reading about, and spending time thinking about.

As the leafy green vegetable of almost any project, money is essential to starting, running, and expanding a business. It's something that all successful entrepreneurs have had to deal with, and that they've disliked intensely at some point in their company's journey from idea to empire. It's something that has caused each successful founder to make mistakes—many, *many* mistakes—over the course of that journey.

Just ask Venus Williams, a woman who knows a thing or two about overcoming setbacks. The Wimbledon champion, US Open champion, and Olympic gold medalist spends her not-very-copious spare time running her startup, sportswear and athleisure maker EleVen by Venus.

In her role as founder and CEO, Williams has faced more than sports injuries and on-court rivalries; she's overcome the bankruptcy of her retail partner and costly manufacturing mistakes. And she managed to recover, and then some, turning her business around so that it tripled sales in 2016.

"I always dreamed of being an entrepreneur," Williams told *Inc.* in 2017. "That was one of my lifelong goals."[2]

If you're reading this book, that dream probably sounds familiar. As will the mistakes that Williams made with money, and that many other successful and prominent entrepreneurs—including Mark Cuban, Bobbi Brown, Jack Ma, Christina Tosi, and Daymond John—all surmounted as they built their businesses.

This book will share their stories, and those of many other startup founders, as it walks you through the biggest money questions you'll face about your business: How much money do you need to start something new? How should you raise the necessary funds, whether from banks or venture capitalists or family and friends? What financial hurdles might you encounter, after your business starts to expand? And maybe even, someday, how can you sell or retire from your business, and enjoy everything that your hard work created?

The answers lie within this guide—along with lots of stories and advice from today's most successful entrepreneurs. If you're looking for some inspiration, and a whole lot of commiseration, you'll find plenty on the pages of this book.

STARTING FROM SCRATCH

" When I was twenty-two years old, a guy who owned a little bodega in my neighborhood told me, 'If you really want to start a company, you better dig under your couch for a couple of extra dollars, stop going out to dinner four times a month, trade in your car for a cheaper one, and raise that $40,000 or $30,000, if you can, by yourself.'"[1]

DAYMOND JOHN, *Shark Tank* investor and FUBU founder

YOU WANT TO START a business. You've got the idea, you're ready to hustle, but how much money do you need to launch your startup?

Ten years ago, the average cost of starting a small business was $31,150, according to one study.[2] That seems laughably large today. While some businesses still require lots of money to get off the ground, at *Inc.*, we regularly hear from founders of fast-growing companies who started their businesses for hundreds, not thousands, of dollars.

"Today a smart entrepreneur with a website can start making in six months what we were making after six years," says Bert Jacobs, cofounder of the apparel company Life Is Good.[3]

Technology's rapid advance is bringing down many startup costs, as Jacobs points out. He and his brother John launched the first iteration of their company in 1989, with $200 borrowed from another brother, Allan. The early days were scrappy, to say the least, as Jacobs told *Inc.*'s Leigh Buchanan:

We would have used that technology if we'd had it. Instead, we spent years building a company with employees we met at pickup basketball games; customers we joked with in the streets while keeping one eye peeled for the beat cop; and advice from retailers up and down the East Coast whom we dropped in on. It may not have been the most effective process. Definitely it wasn't the most efficient. But a lot of our company's values came out of that early need to do things cheap and in person.[4]

Life Is Good now sells $100 million worth of apparel every year. And there are parts of Jacobs's experience, especially the grit and patience, that remain relevant today. If you're dreaming of starting a business that could someday rival his success, you don't necessarily have to spend money in the same ways.

Entrepreneurs who have started their companies more recently agree that the technology of today, well, rocks.

"It's—oh, my god—1,000 percent easier now to go out and set up your own thing," Matthew Schwab, cofounder and president of San Francisco flower-delivery startup BloomThat, told me in 2016.[5]

Schwab set up his company using Stripe, the payment-processing platform that makes it easier for many online businesses to start selling goods or services. And Stripe is just one part of the large ecosystem of tech services that exist to help you get your startup off the ground cheaply and quickly; what we at *Inc.* call the "instant startup kit":

Websites, billing, payment processing, cloud computing, communications, funding—all have been made simpler by the likes of Squarespace, Slack, Kickstarter, Dropbox, Amazon's ubiquitous Web services division, and PayPal. . . .

In the past ten years, these building blocks have greatly reduced the time—and cost—involved to start a business, especially high-tech ones. Thanks to "the emergence of the internet, open-source software, cloud computing, and other trends," some experts estimate tech-reliant ideas "that would have cost $5 million to set up a decade ago can be done for under $50,000 today," according to a 2014 paper from the National Bureau of Economic Research.[6]

Good news: You probably don't need $5 million to start your business! You might not need $50,000 or $30,000. In fact, you might not even need half of that: In 2014, 49 percent of Inc. 500 founders responding to our annual CEO survey[7] said they used under $5,000 to launch their businesses. The next-biggest group, 15 percent, said they needed between $10,000 and $50,000.

The amount of money you need will vary depending on your answers to the following questions:

→ What kind of business do you want to start?

→ How many people do you need to run your startup?

→ Where are you starting your business, and how much space do you need?

→ How quickly do you need to get your product or service to market?

→ How long can you afford to live without a salary?

Let's go through each of these questions.

WHAT KIND OF BUSINESS DO YOU WANT TO START?

This is the most fundamental factor in determining the kind of money you'll need up front: What are you selling, and is it a product or a service?

Product-based businesses tend to be more expensive to initiate. If you're making T-shirts or baking cupcakes or designing mobile apps, you'll need the raw materials to create your product, the equipment for the production, the people to perform the manufacturing or baking or coding, and the space to do the work.

Planning on doing it all yourself, at least at the start? Remember that you'll also need to spend time actually selling your product and marketing it so you'll have customers interested in buying it.

Melissa Ben-Ishay, cofounder of mini-cupcake company Baked by Melissa, got her start during a dark time: The day she was fired from her job as a media planner, in 2008, Ben-Ishay went home and baked two hundred cupcakes. She gave them away to friends to bring into their offices, which piqued caterers' interest. Still, the early days were full of self-doubt and imposter syndrome. Ben-Ishay told me:

> After I was fired from my advertising job, I worked out of my apartment for seven months, by myself. I'd cold-call catering companies and say, "Hi. This is Melissa from Baked by Melissa. I'd like to bring you a free tasting of my cupcakes." I remember crying to my brother, "Who the hell do I think I am?! 'Melissa of Baked by Melissa?'" I felt like a fraud.[8]

Within seven years, Ben-Ishay was selling her cupcakes in fourteen New York–area stores and nationally online.

Inc.com columnist Jason Albanese, cofounder and CEO of digital consultancy Centric Digital, describes the challenge for product-based startups as "up-front product development costs, coupled with the risk of market acceptance. In other words, there's no real way of knowing whether or not the product you're investing in is going to succeed and offer any kind of substantial return."[9]

Service-based businesses are, in many ways, a lot easier and cheaper to launch, particularly if you already have industry expertise and contacts. If you're a lawyer or an accountant or a digital marketing expert or have any other specialized business experience, you have the product (your expertise) and, potentially, the market. You can start selling your services on your own to people and companies that may be familiar with you and your work.

You don't have to hire anyone else, at least at first. You don't necessarily have to spend more money on office space, as long as you can work out of your home. And ideally, you don't have to spend as much time marketing your services.

The downside: Albanese points out that service-based companies face more costs and complexity later on as they try to scale, since their growth depends on having more people. We'll address expansion costs in Chapter 6.

HOW MANY PEOPLE DO YOU NEED TO RUN YOUR STARTUP?

As we discussed above, if you're selling yourself and your services, you'll need less money up front than if you expect to hire others. For product-based businesses, you can do what you can on your own—and you can beg friends and family to help—but it's more likely that you'll soon need to pay for help.

That doesn't necessarily mean bringing on full-time employees; you can also consider hiring consultants or part-time workers. An increasing number of online marketplaces provide one-off help with specific tasks, as well as remote help with recurring work. Freelancer and remote job sites include Upwork (all sorts of freelancers), Working Not Working (creative and design work), and PowerToFly (tech talent, much of it remote and looking for longer-term assignments, specializing in matching tech jobs with qualified women).[10]

If you're planning to start a business that requires full-time employees, your immediate expenses, beyond salaries and healthcare costs, may include other insurance, rent for your workspace, and retirement plans. There are less obvious costs, too, as we will discuss in a later chapter.

WHERE ARE YOU STARTING YOUR BUSINESS, AND HOW MUCH SPACE DO YOU NEED?

Can you work out of your home? Do you need office space, or desks in a coworking space? And are you starting your business in an expensive, densely populated city or in a place with lower real estate costs?

Cities across the Midwest and in the growing tech hubs of Utah are some of the best places to start a business, due in part to their affordable real estate, according to annual rankings by personal-finance website WalletHub.[11]

Meanwhile, the six most expensive cities for office space are all in California, as many a Silicon Valley founder knows, which has led to lots of competition for office space, and some creative cost-saving strategies.

One California-based startup, social-media analytics firm Buffer, tried to save some rent in 2015 by closing its San Francisco office, "since too few employees were using it," *Inc.*'s Victoria Finkle reports. "Instead, the startup covers coworking memberships for those who want them, an estimated 15 to 20 percent" of the startup's then-staff of sixty-four people.[12]

HOW QUICKLY DO YOU NEED TO GET YOUR PRODUCT OR SERVICE TO MARKET?

Do you have a brilliant idea to solve an immediate problem, and will customers still buy your product if you spend months or years developing it? In the meantime, how many competitors will introduce a version of your idea?

If speed is of the essence, you may need outside money—and a lot of it—to quickly develop and start selling your product. This is especially true for consumer-facing, tech-related startups, as the smartphone age upends everything from finding taxis and booking hotels to dating. This was the experience of one group of friends you may have heard of:

Back in 2007, the idea barely got off the ground. [Brian] Chesky and [Joe] Gebbia, newly graduated from the Rhode Island School of Design, were sharing an apartment in San Francisco, struggling to pay the rent. Both had the startup bug but failed to come up with anything mainstream. Then they had an idea. A design conference was coming to town, and they decided to rent out air mattresses on their floor to visitors for $80 a night. They called and emailed every major design firm in San Francisco, asking if anyone else had a room for rent. They built a website, airbedandbreakfast.com, to connect hosts and guests.[13]

Chesky and Gebbia, along with cofounder Nathan Blecharczyk, applied to prominent Silicon Valley accelerator Y Combinator in 2009. They were "desperate for money and ideas," as *Inc.*'s Burt Helm reported—and they soon found both. Within a few years, their young company, now known as Airbnb, had raised billions of dollars and started upending the traditional hotel industry.[14]

By March 2017, the company was the second most valuable private company in the United States, according to research firm CB Insights.[15]

FINALLY, AND MOST IMPORTANT, HOW LONG CAN YOU AFFORD TO LIVE WITHOUT A SALARY?

Becoming your own boss usually means giving yourself a pay cut, or not paying yourself anything at all. Only 25 percent of responding CEOs started paying themselves immediately, according to our 2017 Inc. 500 CEO survey.[16] The largest segment, 32 percent of CEOs, started paying themselves within a year of starting their businesses, and another 20 percent started taking a salary within two years.

Debbie Sterling, founder and CEO of STEM-focused toy company GoldieBlox, realized during a conversation with her then boyfriend (now husband) that the only way to launch her startup would be to focus on it full-time. A Stanford-educated engineer and product designer, Sterling worked in branding at a creative agency, spent six months volunteering in rural India, and handled marketing for a small jewelry-design business before realizing that she had to take the plunge if she ever wanted to launch her idea for girls' STEM (science, technology, engineering, and mathematics) toys.

"I saved as much money as I could, so that I had enough in the bank to last me an entire year, and put all of my attention into GoldieBlox," Sterling told *Inc.*'s Anna Hensel. "Nine months later, I launched a Kickstarter campaign and raised more than $250,000—and I was finally able to give myself my first paycheck as GoldieBlox's CEO."[17]

Once your business starts generating consistent revenue, you can afford to give yourself a paycheck. Even then, keep it low: 40 percent of the CEOs in our 2017 survey started with salaries of less than $50,000.[18] We'll discuss what to pay yourself, and when to start taking a paycheck, in more detail in Chapter 6.

For now, it's important to realize that starting a business probably won't make you rich in the short term. In fact, it's much more likely that it will make you broke.

Which brings us to the biggest and most important disclaimer in this entire book:

||||||||||||||||||||||||||||||||||||||||||||||||||||||||||||||||||||||||||||||||||||||||||||||||||||||||||||||||||||||||

YOUR BUSINESS WILL PROBABLY FAIL.
DON'T SPEND MONEY ON IT YOU CAN'T AFFORD TO LOSE.

||||||||||||||||||||||||||||||||||||||||||||||||||||||||||||||||||||||||||||||||||||||||||||||||||||||||||||||||||||||||

Most businesses fail. Yours probably will. About half of all startups fail within five years, according to the Bureau of Labor Statistics;[19] within ten years, about 70 percent of new businesses have gone bust.

That means you have a high probability of losing any and all money you put into your business. It's like any other risky investment: There are potentially huge upsides, but the downsides are far more statistically likely.

However hard you work or confident you feel, take a minute to think about what your business's failure would mean for your financial situation. Can you afford to lose all the money you put into it? If your startup fails and you can't immediately find another job, will you still be able to pay rent or make payments on your mortgage and your car? Will you be able to feed yourself and your family? If you have children, will you still be able to pay for their care, clothing, and education?

If the answer to any of those questions is no—whatever the cost of starting your business, it's too high.

Before you read further, start saving for a cushion. Sock away enough money to cover your necessary expenses for several months, so that, if your business fails, you can eat and stay in your home and take care of your children.

This is what Alexa von Tobel, founder of financial-planning website LearnVest, calls a "freedom fund." Von Tobel started LearnVest in 2009, after dropping out of Harvard Business School.[20] Six years later, she sold it to Northwestern Mutual for a reported $250 million.[21]

As von Tobel writes in *Inc.*:

> As unnatural as it may feel to invest precious dollars in yourself and not your business . . . if your business ultimately fails, it may take you longer than you expect to find a new job or launch a new venture. Your freedom fund can be a bridge during a transition to help cover your essential bills. And it will let you sleep at night.

If you're single, I recommend you create a freedom fund that covers up to nine months of living expenses, and if you're married, up to a year. If you have children, consider saving more. Yes, those targets are well above the three to six months you may have heard about. That can make sense for folks who work for someone else. But it may not make sense for you.[22]

Once you've socked away this freedom fund, and you can afford to burn other money on starting your business, break the glass and read on. Even if this doesn't make you rich, this will be fun.

Just ask Bobby Flay, the celebrity chef and Food Network star, who once considered giving up cooking for a better paycheck.

"At one point, I quit the restaurant business to go work on Wall Street for about six months, as a clerk at the American Stock Exchange," Flay told *Inc.*'s Christine Lagorio-Chafkin.[23] "But there was no creativity to it. It was all about the dollar. I went back to the kitchen."

He became a household name—and the founder of a company that had launched twenty-seven restaurants by 2015 and employed close to 1,500 people.

Ready to try to beat Bobby Flay, or at least follow his lead into business? Now that you have a rough idea of how much money you'll need to start your business, it's time to figure out how you're going to scrape it together.

From Queens Streets to Shark Tanks

 Daymond John didn't grow up wealthy. He was dyslexic, was held back in school, and says he didn't have many positive role models during his childhood in a lower-middle-class part of Queens, New York.

"I didn't know anybody, didn't have a famous last name, didn't have any access to capital, and didn't go to college," he told *Inc.*'s Emily Canal. "Many people would've said one of those things could have held me back, and none of those held me back."[24]

In 1989, he launched his groundbreaking apparel business by selling hand-sewn hats on the streets of Hollis, Queens. FUBU's early days were heady, but cash-strapped. Twenty-seven banks turned John down for a loan, and FUBU was running out of money to keep the lights on. John's mother came to the rescue in 1995, taking out a second mortgage on the house she and John lived in, for $100,000.

"Early on, I thought that money could solve everything. I thought that access to capital was no problem. The fear wasn't there, because I was too dumb to understand. I didn't have the financial knowledge that I needed," John told *Inc.*'s Zoe Henry. "Once I depleted everything, it was a very scary time. But my mother saw the work I was putting in. . . . She saw that I wouldn't give up."[25]

By the late 1990s, FUBU was doing $150 million in annual sales. It's more like $20 million today, a figure John says he's content with: "I don't want a company with more than one hundred people," he told Henry. "I had it, once. FUBU had gotten up to two hundred employees and change, and externally probably another six hundred people. I wanted to kill myself. You don't know anyone's name anymore."

Not that John lacks for entrepreneurial success these days. A father of three, he's running two other businesses along with FUBU—brand management agency The Shark Group, and coworking space Blueprint + Co.

Of course, he's also one of the original investors and judges on ABC's *Shark Tank*, where he regularly counsels other entrepreneurs on what to do with their money, while sometimes doling out his own. One of the biggest lessons John says he's learned during the course of the show's ten years goes back to his initial mistake: Money, still, can't solve everything. As John told *Inc.*'s Canal:

I had a company that my partners and I were financing, a ladies apparel company [Heatherette], and we spent about $6 million in funding the company. We had to shut it down because we realized we were going to be out of more and more money. The bad part about it was, we had to fire fifteen people and let down the partners we invested in, because they thought that we'd be able to take it to another level. You have to learn from that.

It taught me that unless you have partners who fully know the area of business and they're really good operators, then you can't buy your way into businesses. You have to roll up your sleeves and work just as hard as if it were you starting from the beginning. Most of the businesses I would launch after that, I would start off at a very small level and figure out all the problems, and it ended up saving me a lot more money in the future.[26]

———

BUSINESS PLANNING AND BOOT-STRAPPING

> My mother used to tell me, "You are the only person you can depend on to put food in your mouth." So, in the early days of Mailchimp, it never occurred to me to borrow money or get funding to grow my business. . . . If I need to make more money, I find a way to serve more customers—just like my mother taught me."[1]

BEN CHESTNUT, cofounder and CEO of Mailchimp

ONCE YOU'VE DECIDED TO take the startup plunge, you've got to figure out how much money you'll need up front and how much you'll need as your business grows.

Unfortunately, no set-it-and-forget-it financial fix exists. You'll have to wrestle with money questions as long as you're in business. In 2017, 64 percent of small businesses said they had faced financial challenges within the prior twelve months, according to the Federal Reserve. Paying operating expenses was the biggest challenge for 40 percent of businesses surveyed, followed by finding credit, making debt payments, and purchasing inventory.[2]

Those money problems never completely go away—more than half of small businesses that have been around for sixteen years or longer told the Fed that they still face financial problems—but the problems are notably bad for startups. A whopping 71 percent of new businesses (up to five years old) say that they faced financial problems in the past year.

Sarah Carson, founder and CEO of New York–based dressmaking startup Leota, was one of them. A US champion in full-contact kung fu, Carson became a Wall Street investment banker before deciding to get into dressmaking. She taught herself design and set out to sell Leota's brightly patterned dresses to big department stores.

Three years after launching her company in 2010, sales were skyrocketing. As a former banker, Carson had the experience to make smart financial decisions—which is what she thought she was doing when she decided to double her inventory for the upcoming spring season.

That turned into a $300,000 mistake, as *Inc.*'s Victoria Finkle reports:

> Like many first-time founders still getting a handle on their company's business cycles, Carson had failed to plan for the delay from when she made her products to when she could deliver them—or, more crucially, get paid for them. She didn't realize her mistake until after the fabric had been ordered and the dresses made, creating an inventory pileup. The department stores that are Leota's biggest customers didn't want their shipments for two to three months—long after several bills were due. Which is how, during an explosive sales season that should have been her biggest triumph, Carson suddenly found herself on the hook for $300,000 she didn't have.
>
> "I was scared and embarrassed—I was on the brink of growing the business to failure," Carson recalls. "I had perfectly made dresses hanging on the racks there, ready to go—and I didn't have the cash to pay the vendors who had made them."[3]

Carson called suppliers and manufacturing partners, asking to renegotiate her payment terms, and got a bridge loan from her lender to tide her over. Her hustle and quick thinking paid off: Leota landed on the 2015 and 2016 Inc. 500 lists of the fastest-growing companies in America, with 2015 revenue of $4.3 million.[4]

Planning for these sorts of financial "unknown unknowns," to quote a former US secretary of defense, is tricky. You can't predict every financial challenge your startup will face. Yet you can and should answer some basic financial questions and explore potential scenarios.

Which means it's time to write your business plan.

THE BEGINNER'S GUIDE TO BUSINESS PLANNING

" My mom taught me: Not having a financial plan is a plan—it's just a really bad one!"[5]

—
ALEXA VON TOBEL, founder of LearnVest

Before you start spending money on your business, you need to prove that you have one. Prove it to yourself, yes, but also to any early employees you'll try to recruit, and anyone you're going to ask for money. While your friends and family might not ask to see a business plan before they write you a check, banks and outside investors will.

First and foremost, as von Tobel points out, formalizing your business plan will help you avoid any early or unpleasant surprises. As Inc.com's Jeff Haden writes:

Many business plans are fantasies. That's because many aspiring entrepreneurs see a business plan as simply a tool—filled with strategies and projections and hyperbole—that will convince lenders or investors the business makes sense.

That's a huge mistake.

First and foremost, your business plan should convince you that your idea makes sense—because your time, your money, and your effort are on the line.

So, a solid business plan should be a blueprint for a successful business. It should flesh out strategic plans, develop marketing and sales plans, create the foundation for smooth operations, and maybe—just maybe—convince a lender or investor to jump on board.[6]

This means your business plan should describe what problem you are solving, how your product or service solves it, who will be buying your product or service, why you and any cofounders have the experience to solve this problem, and your financial plan.

Legalese and Business Structures

Also, as long as you're planning, spare a thought for how you want to legally structure your business. Think LLCs, S Corporations, C Corporations, or even the newer B Corporation certification to show your commitment to a social mission.[7]

What you choose will affect the taxes you pay and the liability you'll face in the event of any lawsuits. So—and this is only one of many times we'll say this throughout this book—please consult financial and legal experts before making a decision.

Traditionally, most small businesses have been structured as "pass-through" entities such as limited liability companies (LLCs) or S Corporations, where profits are taxed according to the owner's personal rate. Nevertheless, recent tax law changes, which cap the corporate tax rate for C Corporations at 21 percent instead of 35 percent, are causing many small businesses to think about reclassifying, *Inc.*'s Zoe Henry reports.[8] Pass-through firms also have some tax relief, including a temporary ability to deduct up to 20 percent of income, but that will expire in 2025, unless Congress extends it.[9]

"I do believe it's an amazing loophole," Anne Zimmerman, founder and CEO of the Cincinnati-based small-businesses accounting firm Zimmerman and Co., told Henry, adding that she is advising some of her clients to convert to C Corporations.[10]

However, that conversion can also be a bit of a hassle and a time suck. As Henry reports, to convert your company to a C Corporation, "generally, you need to file a set of articles of incorporation with the secretary of state's office; draft a series of corporate bylaws; and elect corporate officers and directors. You also need to hold annual board meetings and issue stock certificates."[11]

Make sure your business is at the stage that's worth taking on that complexity, and again, please first consult your lawyer and your accountant.

The Basics of Business Planning

There are many different ways to write a business plan, and many different models. Make it easy on yourself and follow one of the thousands of free templates available online. For example, the Small Business Administration website has samples of both a traditional plan and a stripped-down "lean startup" plan,[12] while business-planning website Bplans.com has templates and plenty of other resources for entrepreneurs at this stage of startup planning.[13] So does small-business-mentoring nonprofit SCORE.[14]

You can also pay for business-planning software. And it wouldn't hurt to consult your accountant, banker, and/or financial advisor. As Inc.com's Jeff Haden points out, you shouldn't fully outsource all of your financial planning: "While you don't need to be an accountant to run a business, you do need to understand your numbers," he writes. "And the best way to understand your numbers is usually to actually work with your numbers."[15]

A business plan is about more than just your finances. You'll need to describe your product or service, your customer base, and how you plan to market and sell your product or service. But the financial section is probably the most important part of the plan.

As Elizabeth Wasserman writes in *Inc.*'s extensive online guide to writing a business plan's financial section, "The sections about your marketing plan and strategy are interesting to read, but they don't mean a thing if you can't justify your business with good figures on the bottom line."[16] She continues:

> The financial section of a business plan is one of the most essential components of the plan, as you will need it if you have any hope of winning over investors or obtaining a bank loan. Even if you don't need financing, you should compile a financial forecast in order to simply be successful in steering your business.
>
> "This is what will tell you whether the business will be viable or whether you are wasting your time and/or money," says Linda Pinson, author of *Automate Your Business Plan for Windows* (Out of Your Mind 2008) and *Anatomy of a Business Plan* (Out of Your Mind 2008), who runs a publishing and software business Out of Your Mind and Into the Marketplace. "In many instances, it will tell you that you should not be going into this business." ...
>
> The most important reason to compile this financial forecast is for your own benefit, so you understand how you project your business will do. "This is an ongoing, living document.

It should be a guide to running your business," Pinson says. "And at any particular time you feel you need funding or financing, then you are prepared to go with your documents."[17]

The essential elements your business plan's financial section should include are the following:

→ **Cash-flow statement,** or a projection of cash receipts and expense payments. Fundamentally: How and when will your business get paid, and how and when will you have to spend money?

→ **Income statement (aka profit/loss statement),** or a projection of revenues minus expenses. How profitable will your business be in a given period?

→ **Balance sheet,** or a summary of your business's overall financial situation, including cash, assets (land, buildings, equipment), and liabilities (debts).

→ **Sales forecast,** or your projections for how much you'll be able to sell over the next few years.

→ **Break-even analysis,** or your projection of how long it will take your business to become profitable.[18]

When you're just starting out, these numbers all rely on assumptions. They will inevitably change, and you'll have to update your plan to reflect those changes. Just don't "set it and forget it." As Wasserman reports:

One of the biggest mistakes businesspeople make is to look at their business plan, and particularly the financial section, only once a year. "I like to quote former President Dwight D. Eisenhower," says [Tim Berry, founder of Palo Alto Software and Bplans.com, and author of several books about business planning]. "'The plan is useless, but planning is essential.' What people do wrong is focus on the plan, and once the plan is done, it's forgotten. It's really a shame, because they could have used it as a tool for managing the company." In fact, Berry recommends that business executives sit down with the business plan once a month and fill in the actual numbers in the profit and loss statement and compare those numbers with projections. And then use those comparisons to revise projections in the future.[19]

But forget about facts, figures, and finances for a minute. Putting in the work to compile your business plan, and thinking through how you're going to have to spend money to make money, can give you the opportunity to seek advice from fellow entrepreneurs, mentors, and potential advisors.

As Nathaniel Ru, cofounder of salad chain Sweetgreen, told *Inc.*'s Leigh Buchanan and Sheila Marikar:

> In the first days of being an entrepreneur, you need guidance and advice from other entrepreneurs. They'll tell you if you're on the right track. And they'll compel you to think beyond your immediate survival to the company you want to have two years from now.
>
> At the very least, you'll want an experienced eye to look over your business plan, if you decide to do one. At Sweetgreen, our mentors (the three of us each had three to five) asked a lot of tough, helpful questions—about our financial model, our brand positioning, our restaurant design, and more.

But they also urged us to look up from the frenetic day-to-day activity and think more long term about our mission and the language we'd use to communicate it. They started us thinking early about the kinds of people we'd want to bring on board one day, so we'd be able to spot great talent even if we weren't ready to hire.[20]

By the beginning of 2018, more than ten years after it launched out of its cofounders' Georgetown dorm rooms, Sweetgreen had established more than eighty restaurants in several big US cities, hired more than four thousand employees at those salad shops, and raised $135 million from investors, including Shake Shack founder Danny Meyer, Momofuku overlord David Chang, and prolific French restaurateur Daniel Boulud.[21]

Which brings us to bootstrapping. It's a funny bit of jargon that means pulling yourself up by your bootstraps, Horatio Alger style. Practically, it means that your startup doesn't accept money from outside investors. Which, of course, means you don't have to accept any of their strings either—the equity stake, outside pressure to do something you don't want to do, the eventual pressure to sell or go public from those looking to get their payday—or, conversely, waiting on someone else's schedule to jump ahead with your business.

Matt Maloney and Mike Evans were working as developers at Apartments.com, building search tools for residential real estate, when they got frustrated by how annoying and time-consuming it was to order dinner at the office. Options were few, and calling the restaurants to read off complicated orders and credit card numbers was a pain. Soon, Evans had a eureka moment: What if he took the search tools he was building for real estate, and built something similar for online restaurant delivery?

Maloney and Evans collected hundreds of menus around Chicago, wrote some code, and convinced restaurants to pay them a 10 percent commission on food deliveries placed through what's now known as Grubhub. After that, Maloney told *Inc.*'s Liz Welch, they tried to convince investors to back their expansion:

> We realized we had a really good product that was scalable. The next step was expanding to a second city. We tried to raise venture capital to do that, but it was taking too long. VCs are slow to say yes, but they'll never say no. The longer they can push you off, the more options they keep open. So, we said, "Screw it! We're going to do it anyway." We flew out to San Francisco to sign up restaurants and do guerrilla marketing. We bootstrapped, and it paid off. The restaurants were really receptive, and the orders started coming in aggressively. People in San Francisco loved it, and investors noticed. We opened in San Francisco in October 2007 and closed our first capital round that November.[22]

Chicago-based Grubhub made the Inc. 500 in 2010 and 2011, then merged with competitor Seamless and raised nearly $200 million in a 2014 IPO (initial public offering). Fourteen years after its launch, Maloney is now the CEO of a company that makes $683 million in annual revenue.

Still, bootstrapping has its downsides: It's lonely, it's hard, it can mean you don't have expert advice or connections, and it definitely means you don't have the sudden infusion of capital that can help jump-start your business. Though challenging, it's the safest, and often the smartest, way to get started. As *Inc.*'s Tom Foster writes:

For bootstrappers, getting ahead of themselves is not a financially viable option. "Bootstrapping means focusing on cash flow, minimizing expenses, and maximizing accounts receivable," says Rachel Everett, the founder of Viderity (No. 68), a Washington, DC–based consultancy that provides IT services for public-sector clients. (She started it with $3,000.) She calls that devotion to the most basic Business 101 principles "an inherent self-control mechanism for growth."

What's more, Inc. 500 bootstrappers believe that self-funding creates a different, more fundamentally sound kind of company—more frugal, customer-focused, and bottom-line driven from Day One. And they get to keep all the equity.

Of course, these founders earned every penny of that equity. Bootstrapping is legendarily hard, requiring sacrifices that most people wouldn't dream of making. Surely, in their darkest moments, these CEOs must have considered giving up some equity for money and peace of mind. But they never did it.[23]

In 2015, 48 percent of 750 respondents polled on Inc.com said a reason for not starting a company yet was, "I don't think I could raise enough money."[24] Even if you decide to seek venture financing later, you'll probably have to scramble on your own in the beginning.

That's what Michael Dubin did, when he decided to start his men's razor subscription service, Dollar Shave Club. With a background in media and marketing, Dubin also spent eight years doing improv training with the Upright Citizens Brigade. When a friend's father needed help offloading a surplus of men's razors, Dubin was inspired to start his company—and, crucially, to market it with a YouTube video that quickly went viral:

I did the bulk of Dollar Shave Club's creative work in the beginning. I wrote the script for that first video spot, and a friend of mine from my improv days shot it in one day for $4,500. It was very scrappy. The day it went live, our site crashed from all the traffic—but within 48 hours, we received 12,000 orders.[25]

Within four years, Dubin turned Dollar Shave Club into a company selling $225 million worth of razors and other grooming products, with an in-house creative agency—and sold the company to Unilever for a reported $1 billion.

Bootstrapping can seem unfashionable in high-tech or high-profile Silicon Valley circles. There's often a perception that, by refusing outside investment, you're dooming your company to small, limited, local success.

That's hardly the case for some successful founders of high-profile companies, including S'well ($100 million revenue in 2016), Mailchimp ($500 million revenue in 2017), and GT's Kombucha ($300 million revenue in 2014).

S'well founder Sarah Kauss, for example, is a self-described "recovering accountant" who set out in 2010 to design beautiful, but also super-functional, water bottles. She never took outside investment, instead hustling to get her bottles into trade shows and independent retailers.

In 2011, a call from the Oprah empire jump-started S'well's expansion, *Inc.*'s Kimberly Weisul reports:

When an editor for *O, The Oprah Magazine* asked Kauss to provide her with "all" of S'well's colors—at the time ocean blue was the only one the company produced—she scrambled to broaden the line's range. Her small staff were mostly, as she describes them, "fashionistas," and had the instinct to make bets on colors like rose gold two months before Apple made an iPhone of the same color (Apple then asked S'well to sell those bottles in its Cupertino store). S'well bottles can now be found in 2,600 specialty shops, high-end department stores like Neiman Marcus and Nordstrom, and athleisure chains like Athleta.[26]

By June 2017, Kauss was selling her bottles in sixty-five countries and overseeing a company that made $100 million revenue in 2016.

Another bootstrapped bottle-related business, GT's Kombucha, was started by a then seventeen-year-old who now goes by GT Dave. In 2015, *Inc.*'s Tom Foster profiled GT and called him "The King of Kombucha," then a $600 million industry:

> The story may also be seen as one of extraordinary bootstrapped growth. Before GT's, there was no such thing as commercial kombucha. According to an *Inc.* analysis, this year consumers will buy $600 million worth of the fizzy stuff—that roughly equals the US market for coconut water—and more than half will be GT's. The category, which started in local health-food markets and went national thanks to Whole Foods, has now spread to Safeway and even Walmart. GT owns 100 percent of the company, and has taken out only one loan, $10,000 from [his mother,] Laraine. And he's never bought an ad, preferring to let the product speak for itself—which it does rather effectively when it shows up in the hands of Madonna, Gwyneth Paltrow, Reese Witherspoon, and other paparazzi targets.[27]

If you're planning to bootstrap your business, where do you find the initial money?

WHERE TO FIND YOUR FUNDING

While much less glamorous than venture capital (VC), plenty of non-VC startup financing sources exist. Three-quarters of Inc. 500 founders responding to our annual CEO survey in 2014 said they used their savings to start their business; 43 percent took out loans from banks, friends, or family; and just 22 percent used venture or angel capital.[28]

The sections that follow will explain the most common startup financing sources.

Savings

Like any other big, expensive life goal—a house, a big wedding, college tuition, getting out of debt—your startup is something you should plan ahead to fund. Start setting aside money now, if you haven't already, and consider these steps to help build your business savings:

Keep costs down. We hear this a lot from successful startup founders, especially when we ask them to pass on the best financial advice they were ever given.

"My dad told me that keeping my personal spending low would give me more flexibility than I ever imagined in my career," Zach Perret, cofounder and CEO of financial startup Plaid, told *Inc.*'s Anna Hensel. "We spent a long time bootstrapping in the early days, and having a low burn rate was very important."[29]

Of course, some dads of successful founders have different advice—which has worked out just as well.

Just ask cosmetics empire builder Bobbi Brown, who moved to New York in 1980 with a degree in theatrical makeup and an amateur portfolio. Over the next several years, as she worked as a freelance makeup artist and started introducing the more natural beauty look that her eventual company would be known for, Brown practiced moderation in her budgeting habits, too.

"When I was just starting my career in New York, my father told me, 'Don't waste your time trying to stick to a budget. Figure out how to make more money,'" Brown told *Inc.*'s Anna Hensel. "'And always spend money on good food.'"[30]

Brown and her business partner, Rosalind Landis, started Bobbi Brown Cosmetics with $10,000. She networked at magazine shoots and dinner parties, once bluffing Bergdorf Goodman into a bidding war with Saks over which department store got to carry her products. Brown sold her company to Estée Lauder in 1995, but stayed with the brand for the next two decades.[31]

By the time she stepped down, Brown had created a makeup empire with thousands of employees, millions of dollars of revenue, and a reputation for doing business by being nice to people.

"It's common sense," Brown told an audience at a 2017 *Inc.* event. "Don't do it because you want something. [Do it because] it actually makes you feel good."[32]

Which brings us to the best way to boost your savings:

Work for someone else and build your startup nest egg, the same way you might plan and save toward a mortgage down payment or other big life goal. That's how Kathryn Minshew, CEO and cofounder of The Muse, worked toward starting her company:[33]

Early on in my career, . . . one of my mentors advised me not to accept a job offer as a management consultant because my spending habits would inevitably adapt to the high salary and, in his view, would lock me into always needing an expensive lifestyle. While it was a smart warning, I've always believed that getting used to any financial changes is a choice more than a default . . . I ended up accepting the position and lived well below my means, which allowed me to save enough money to eventually start my own company. That experience now informs the advice I give people: The more you're able to live an adaptable financial lifestyle, especially early in your career or in advance of a potential career change, the more flexibility and freedom you give yourself to find the right path—not just one that hits a certain tax bracket.[34]

Working for a bigger company can also occasionally provide windfalls in the form of bonuses or stock options, which is what helped Therese Tucker, founder and CEO of accounting-software company BlackLine.

Tucker is one of the only women founders (and probably the only pink-haired founder) to take a modern tech company public—which she did after years of working for other tech companies:

Rather than try to raise money from venture capitalists, Tucker cashed out her retirement accounts and her SunGard options and took out a second mortgage on her house. At forty, with more than fifteen years of experience programming for financial companies, she had both the contacts and the professional seasoning, yet she still had to prove her qualifications. In meetings with early clients or potential investors, Tucker often heard "remarks like, 'Oh, well, your husband's support-ing you, right?'" recalls Charlie Gaulke, a woman Tucker hired as BlackLine's fifth employee and who is now vice president of development. "She did so much of it with her own financial backing, her own sheer will and determination."[35]

BlackLine landed on the Inc. 5000 list of the fastest-growing private companies in America nine consecutive times, from 2008 to 2016, when Tucker oversaw its $152 million IPO. In 2017, the company reported $177 million in revenue.

Tucker also financed her startup's early days with a risky, but not uncommon, financial decision:

Tap your 401(k)s or other retirement accounts. This tends to be a bad idea, since you'll destroy your retirement safety net, but that hasn't stopped many a founder from taking the risk. You'll also have to pay a high tax burden to take money out of tax-sheltered financial accounts—meaning that the dollar amount you're able to take out may be far less than what you see in there today. Therefore, we don't advise this strategy. If you decide to do it anyway, first consult a financial advisor or accountant.

Loans

   Right now is actually quite a good time for small businesses to borrow, but getting a loan that works for you and is affordable and has terms you can understand is still a challenge."[36]

KAREN MILLS, former head of the Small Business Administration under President Obama and a senior fellow at Harvard Business School

Ten years after the financial crisis, when banks stopped lending or shut their doors completely, it's starting to get easier to secure a small-business loan. Banks and credit card companies are lending again—and a wide array of online-only lenders have sprung up, offering quicker (though often more expensive) credit. Let's go through your top options:

Bank and/or SBA Loans

These are some of the safest, smartest, and cheapest ways to fund your business. They're also some of the most difficult to get. Almost half of small businesses applied to large or small banks for credit in 2017, but of all businesses seeking debt financing, 54 percent did not get all the credit they applied for, according to the Federal Reserve.[37]

You'll have a better chance of securing a bank loan if you have a good personal credit score and an existing relationship with a financial institution. Look around for local banks or credit unions, where loan officers may have more time to get to know you or have more incentive to take a risk on a local business owner. Also, ensure your paperwork is in order.

"Whether or not your bank knows you, you won't get money if you don't have a formal business plan and up-to-date paperwork," *Inc.* "Spread the Wealth" columnist Helaine Olen advises. "The bank will likely want to see business-related financial statements for the past three to five years or personal financial records. Be prepared to personally guarantee the loan, even if it's for a business."[38]

Now, aren't you glad you wrote that business plan?

You'll need it if you want to apply for SBA loans, which Inc. com columnist and debt-financing advisor Ami Kassar calls "the lending world gold standard."[39] These bank loans are guaranteed by the US government's Small Business Administration, at low interest rates or with lengthy repayment terms and other benefits.

The government doesn't lend the money directly, and it caps the total amount of SBA loans it can guarantee every year. There are also restrictions on the types of businesses that can apply and the loans they can get. The SBA's website (sba.gov) has more information about the program, and your banker or financial advisor should be able to help walk you through an application.

Credit Cards

 Don't use credit cards."[40]

—

MARK CUBAN, *Shark Tank* investor and owner of the Dallas Mavericks

Credit cards can get you into a lot of trouble, and a lot of debt. We hear this over and over again when we ask successful founders for their biggest money mistakes.

In college, "they were letting everyone sign up for credit cards, and I think that was my first big lesson that just because you can get access to money doesn't mean you should take it," Away co-founder Jen Rubio told me at *Inc.*'s 2017 Women's Summit. "That little personal lesson there has really given me a lot more diligence in how we run our finances as a business."[41]

Mark Cuban, billionaire owner of the Dallas Mavericks and celebrity investor on *Shark Tank*, spent most of his twenties living on macaroni and cheese and driving a $200 car. And today he tells other entrepreneurs to live as frugally as possible, and to avoid the debt traps that credit cards can become:

"Save your money. Save as much money as you possibly can. Every penny you can," Cuban says. "Instead of coffee, drink water. Instead of going to McDonald's, eat mac and cheese. Cut up your credit cards. If you use a credit card, you don't want to be rich. The first step to getting rich requires discipline."[42]

Max Levchin, cofounder of PayPal and lending startup Affirm, realized the downsides of credit cards the hard way:

> When I was going to school in Chicago, I got one of these old-school department store cards—and went from getting 10 percent off on jeans to owing more than $500 and getting calls from collectors. Ultimately, I was able to pay it off, but I felt guilty throughout—and I learned that something that's too good to be true is never a possibility in the real world.[43]

Credit card interest rates can spiral you into debt quickly, which will wreck your personal credit, even if you use a business card. Bank loans have lower interest rates, but, boy, do they take a lot of time and paperwork (and rejection!) to get, which is why so many entrepreneurs end up putting business expenses on their personal credit cards.

Justin Woolverton, cofounder of Eden Creamery, maker of the low-calorie ice cream Halo Top, is still recovering from his credit card mistakes. Since 2013, when his company made $230,000 in annual revenue, Halo Top has exploded, becoming profitable and making more than $100 million in 2017 revenue.

To make ends meet in his business's early days, Woolverton maxed out five credit cards, racking up a balance of $150,000. When he got turned down for an expensive business loan—with a 24.9 percent interest rate—his cofounder applied for it instead.

Which made Halo Top's eventual success all the sweeter, as *Inc.*'s Burt Helm reports:

In a little less than two years, Halo Top's relentless sales growth has afforded the founders something most entrepreneurs only dream of: They run a profitable company, at scale. They retain majority control. Their debts are paid off. "My credit score is finally above 600," says Woolverton.[44]

Woolverton is hardly alone in turning to credit cards to fund his company. In 2017, 31 percent of small-business owners used credit cards to finance their businesses, according to the National Small Business Association's year-end economic report. That was the second-most-popular type of financing, after the business's earnings.[45]

If you are going to start putting business expenses on your credit card, especially if you're not going to repay the balance in full every month, look for one that won't charge you interest for the first year. Then pay attention to when that 0 percent introductory offer is up. As Fundera cofounder and CEO Jared Hecht writes on Inc.com:

This seems like one of the best business funding deals out there because it is—even the most desirable term loans include some sort of interest, even if it's a low rate.

However, what about when that introductory offer is up? The interest rate will rocket skyward—and you may be unprepared for it. Most credit cards have APRs of at least 13 percent, with some as high as 20 percent. This means financing your business with a credit card could prove to be more expensive in the long term than finding funding through a small-business loan.[46]

Then keep close track of your spending. If you're charging more on your credit card than your business is allowing you to repay, it's probably time to rethink how much money you're spending on starting your business.

Online and "Alternative" Lenders

Speaking of high interest rates, handle this next group of lenders with care. They'll lend to almost anyone, for a price. The interest rates and repayment terms will be worse than bank loans, and typically worse than credit cards.

On the other hand, online lenders will often get you money faster, with far less paperwork, than traditional banks and credit unions—and in many cases, they'll lend to you when banks won't. That's why 24 percent of small businesses applied for online loans in 2017, up from 20 percent in 2015, according to the Federal Reserve: "Applicants tended to choose a lender based on their perceived chance of being funded, rather than on product cost," the Fed concluded.[47]

Many types of lenders are in this group, including two of the more commonly used ones:

→ **Tech-savvy newcomers,** including Lending Club, OnDeck, and Kabbage, some of which specialize in small-business lending. They tend to offer bank-like loans, but often with higher interest rates.

→ **Factoring companies,** which, for a fee, give you cash up front while you're waiting to sell your product. When you do sell your product, your lender receives your sales.

There's a whole Wild West of alternative lenders, including merchant cash-advance providers, which can range from the useful to the predatory. Don't take out any loans you don't understand or can't afford to repay.

At *Inc.*, we've talked to entrepreneurs who have used both online lenders and factoring companies and are happy with the outcomes. Leota's Sarah Carson is one such founder:

> The other thing Carson did while scrambling for cash flow in 2014 was contact her lender, and prepare a detailed presentation explaining her budget crunch. She relies on factoring, a common type of financing for manufacturing-based businesses, in which a company gets up-front cash by selling the factor its accounts receivable (the amounts due from customers). You pay for that quick financing though. It can be pricey, and factors are generally less regulated than traditional bank lenders. But for Carson, it paid off, because her lenders had run into this type of situation before—and they considered her business a good bet. "To my surprise and relief, the factors were not the least bit concerned," she says. "In fact, they wanted to invest in my company's growth. They approved a bridge loan on the spot and wrote me the check that day for the full amount."[48]

Even so, be aware that you're paying for the convenience, and read the terms carefully or consult a financial advisor before taking out any online loans.

Friends and Family Loans

Getting financially involved with friends and family members can be perilous, but it's also gotten many a founder out of a money shortfall. As Food52 cofounder Amanda Hesser recounted to *Inc.*'s Jon Fine, a loan from her husband and her cofounder's mother helped save her startup in the summer of 2010:

> "We were like, 'Do we have to stop this? Are we going to shut this down?'" Hesser recalls. But they didn't. How did they get through it? "Grit," Hesser shoots back. "You have to have the 'this can't fail' feeling."[49]

Both family members have been paid back, and Food52 went on to raise $9 million from investors. In the next chapter, we'll further discuss the perils and payoffs of asking friends and family for money.

Other Bootstrapping Money Tricks

Crowdfunding on sites like Kickstarter or Indiegogo is a relatively new fundraising method. It tends to work best when you're using it to sell a product or to drum up backing for a defined project, rather than for a general help-my-business-grow fund. That way you can give rewards to your investors, like T-shirts, tickets to your movie, or versions of the product once you start making it.

Rewards-based crowdfunding "makes sure we're getting the right product to sell at retail, and builds an early fan base," Helen Greiner, founder of drone startup CyPhy Works, told *Inc.*'s Jennifer Alsever. "It's a way to know we're selling the right product."[50]

Crowdfunding platform fees can be high, and in some cases there's an "all-or-nothing" model—if you don't meet your goal, you'll lose any money you did raise in that campaign.

Also, if you're using rewards-based crowdfunding to presell your product, make sure you're ready to manufacture as many items as you sell. That's a lesson Debbie Sterling of GoldieBlox learned the hard way, according to *Inc.*'s Kimberly Weisul:

> After GoldieBlox finished its Kickstarter campaign, it found itself committed to delivering 40,000 items all at once, which meant there was time for only one [manufacturing] run. Said Sterling, "In retrospect, that's crazy."[51]

Even more complicated is "equity crowdfunding," which allows you to sell shares in your company to nonaccredited investors. Companies including Chicken Soup for the Soul have successfully raised money this way, though it remains a decidedly intermediate-to-advanced-level method of startup financing.

You may know *Chicken Soup for the Soul* as the book series written by motivational speakers Jack Canfield and Mark Victor Hansen. They sold the brand in 2008, and when Chicken Soup took its video and entertainment unit public in an August 2017 offering that raised $30 million, CEO William J. Rouhana had spent hundreds of thousands of dollars on legal and accounting fees to figure out the crowdfunding process.

"Many times when there was a legal question, we were in brand new territory," he told *Inc.*'s Victoria Finkle. "That slowed the process down and probably made it more expensive."[52]

Still, if you have the stomach, the money, and the patience to figure out the equity crowdfunding market, Rouhana wants you to give it a try. "I hope more businesses will consider this type of funding in the future," he told Finkle. "This is something that is worth continuing to make better."[53]

Finally, there's always *the barter method*. Can you get one of your customers to give you rent-free office space in exchange for your services, as Inc. 5000 company Build Group did for eighteen months?[54] Or like Jacques Torres, founder of a chocolate empire, did?

"Since I didn't have much money, I negotiated with the building owner to give me the space rent-free for a year and a half," Torres told *Inc.*'s Liz Welch about finding his company's first Brooklyn space.[55] That was only the start of the bartering:

> Then, I met with an architect who wanted $600,000 to renovate it. My budget was $150,000. I thought I was out of business before I had even started. But a chef friend who also works as a contractor offered to help. We worked every day for three months—putting in new floors, walls, windows, and a drop ceiling. I used what was left to buy a few pieces of equipment.[56]

By 2013, Torres's company had grown so much he was able to spend $3.4 million building his own 40,000-square-foot "dream chocolate factory."

Bootstrapping forever isn't for everyone, and you may want to grow faster than you can finance on your own. If that's the case, turn to Chapter 4, in which we'll discuss your options for seeking outside financing.

Remember that, sometimes, years of patience and grit and willingness to continue bootstrapping can pay off beyond your wildest dreams. Just ask Ben Chestnut and Dan Kurzius, cofounders of quirky email-marketing empire Mailchimp.

"I love when there's a problem to solve," Chestnut, Mailchimp's CEO, told me. "I love it when my brows are furrowed."[57]

The child of an army code breaker and a Thai cook, Chestnut grew up sweeping the floors of the hair salon his mother set up in their Georgia home. He also witnessed his older sister struggle with a business she started before declaring bankruptcy—an experience he shared with Kurzius, the son of a baker whose store shuttered. Kurzius blames the stress of that business failure for contributing to his father's fatal heart attack when the Mailchimp cofounder was twelve.

Yet both men remained drawn to startups. After working together at an MP3 business that eventually failed, Chestnut and Kurzius launched a web design company that created what was initially meant to be an email greeting card feature. The web design business never quite found its footing, but the email tool, which the founders turned into a marketing and newsletter function, took off.

Wary of expanding too fast or committing to partners who didn't understand the business, Mailchimp's founders never took outside money. They turned down the VCs who, after some initial success (and the IPO of a competitor), came knocking on their doors. After nearly eighteen years of scraping by and funding their expansion only with what they earned from the business, they turned Mailchimp into a profitable tech company with $525 million in annual revenue and more than seven hundred employees.

In 2017, *Inc.* named Mailchimp Company of the Year, recognizing Chestnut's refusal to take the fast or easy route to success. As I wrote then:

> It took more than five years for Mailchimp to find its sweet spot, and about a decade for Chestnut to feel like it was starting to succeed. That experience influences how he chooses which founders he mentors now. "If they say, 'These hackathons are hard. Do you have advice on how to build a deck?' I don't want to talk to them," he says. "When they've hit some

really tough time—struggling to deal with a partner who's un-cooperative, the real struggles of the small-business owner—those are the ones that I invite in."[58]

Some of those real struggles—and some of your most crucial financial and emotional support—will come from your close friends and family members. For a guide on how to handle startup money and your loved ones, turn to the next chapter.

FRIENDS, FAMILY, AND FINANCES

> " We always say: Don't do this if there is any other option. There wasn't for us. . . . A startup is like a child: You protect your child over your spouse. But eventually you have to say, 'Wait. The whole thing falls apart if our marriage doesn't last.'"[1]

CARLEY RONEY, cofounder (with her husband, David Liu) of The Knot, now XO Group

IT'S NOT BUSINESS, IT'S personal. But what happens when it's both?

Starting a business will inevitably involve asking your loved ones for support—emotional, financial, business-related, and often all of the above. So how do you ask friends and family for money for your business? What should you promise them, and what should you avoid? And if you're starting a business together, what financial conversations should you have up front?

Don't mix business with family. Don't ask friends for money. These normal rules tend to go out the window for a lot of small-business owners. After all, if you're starting a business with someone else, you probably want to know and trust them first, right?

And that worked out well for plenty of founders: Drybar's Alli Webb and her brother, Michael Landau; Bluemercury's Marla Malcolm Beck and her husband, Barry Beck; the college or business school friends who started Sweetgreen and Warby Parker; the Collison brothers who started Stripe and an earlier software company that made them teenage millionaires when they sold it for $5 million.[2]

Maysara Winery founder Moe Momtazi fled his native Iran with his wife, Flora, in 1982. After starting and selling a firm, he and his family moved to Oregon in 1990, where Momtazi bought five hundred acres for what is now Momtazi Vineyard, which makes coveted pinot noirs and grossed more than $2 million in 2017. And he's turned it into a family affair, Momtazi told *Inc.'s* Jane Porter:

> We had our three daughters work in the vineyard pruning, mowing—doing a lot of manual labor to teach them a work ethic. My oldest daughter went to Oregon State and studied food science and fermentation. After she graduated in 2006, she became our winemaker. My other daughters work for the winery in sales and marketing.[3]

Still, involving family means a lot can go wrong—whether you're starting a business together, asking your loved ones for money, or using any joint finances to help fund your startup. Let's discuss the three main ways your loved ones and your finances will intersect when you're starting a business—and the work you'll need to do to safeguard your personal ties in each situation.

STARTING A BUSINESS— WHAT IT MEANS FOR YOUR FAMILY FINANCES

If you're not young, single, and childless, any business failure risks hurting more than your personal finances.

"I spent countless nights. After my wife would fall asleep, I literally would get up and go into another bedroom and just lay there awake, because I was so frightened about our finances. In-tears frightened," Rob Frohwein, CEO and cofounder of online lender Kabbage, recently told me:

One time, I was waiting on a $500 check. Shouldn't be a lot of money for a guy that was my age, and had all these expenses. It finally came in the mail. I put it on the kitchen counter, and left the room for like twenty minutes. I came back, and the check was gone.

My wife hadn't seen it. So, I find myself, five minutes later, digging through the trash outside. My wife had been cutting up raw chicken. I found the check laying in that Styrofoam thing [that holds raw chicken]—it was all stained, and I peel it off and take it inside, try to dab it as dry as I can. I was able to deposit it.

So, I was literally digging through trash because I was out of money. I still remember that to this day.[4]

Things improved for Frohwein, who cofounded Kabbage in 2009 with two friends. The online lender is now a three-time Inc. 500 honoree, with $172 million revenue in 2016. That's the best-case scenario.

Meg Cadoux Hirshberg is an expert on mixing business with loved ones; she's the author of *For Better or for Work: A Survival Guide for Entrepreneurs and Their Families,* and she's married to Gary Hirshberg, cofounder of yogurt company Stonyfield Organic. As she told *Inc.*'s Leigh Buchanan and Sheila Marikar:

In all the euphoria of a startup, it's easy to discount that you're putting your family's financial well-being in jeopardy. People talk about entrepreneurs starting their businesses with "personal savings." But those savings are often held in common with a spouse, who may have wanted them for vacation or to draw on while he returned to school. The spouse is also affected if the founder leaves her job and a chunk of the family's income disappears. Even if the founder is nonworking, she may have been responsible for child care.[5]

How can you safeguard your family finances, while following your dreams? According to Cadoux Hirshberg, it starts with excellent communication. She recommends that you and your spouse take these steps before you launch your business:

→ **Sit down together before you start the business,** to calculate how much you can afford to invest in your company; how you'll recoup any lost income while you focus on your business; and, if necessary, what you and your family will do for health insurance while you're focusing on your business.

→ **Schedule regular business meetings** to discuss updates to your income and spending on the business.

→ **Respect your partner's limits** on the maximum unexpected spending on the business. As Cadoux Hirshberg puts it, "Another $25,000? OK. A second mortgage? No."[6]

Pressuring your partner to spend more money than he or she feels comfortable with, spending that money without admitting it, or run-of-the-mill business struggles also risk exacerbating any personal tensions you might have with family members, especially your spouse or romantic partner. A 2012 study published in *Family Relations* and cited by *Inc.*'s Jessica Bruder finds that "couples who argue primarily about money are more likely to get divorced than those who fight mostly about sex, in-laws, chores, or other highly charged topics."[7]

Some entrepreneurs' money woes create lasting damage to their families, their marriages, and even their personal credit. Bruder reports on one worst-case scenario:

"I basically jeopardized the family's finances to fund my startup," says Penelope Trunk of her third company, Brazen Careerist, which hosted virtual job recruiting events. "We cashed out our 401(k)s. We ran out of money twice. We had the electricity turned off."

At one point, the family was living in a 400-square-foot New York City apartment, and Trunk, her husband, and two young sons all slept on the floor. "If twenty-three-year-old guys are sleeping on the floor in Cambridge, no one even cares, right? The Reddit guy slept on the floor," she says. "But I made my family sleep on the floor, so I could get my company off the ground. When I think about that . . ." Her voice trails off.

By the time Trunk and the father of her children divorced, after fourteen years together, she had ruined both of their credit scores.[8]

Not ideal, right? And, as Bruder reports, divorce can also harm your business, since several states "have community property laws that dictate all assets accumulated by the couple during the marriage be split down the middle. That includes company stock. In some cases, companies have been sold to raise cash to pay off spouses. In others, brawling exes have been forced to become business partners."[9]

If you're starting a business while married—either with or without your personal partner—financial advisor Dianne Hively suggests protecting both of you with paperwork. She recommends the following:

→ **If you're not married yet,** sign a prenuptial agreement to declare your business nonmarital property—in other words, a separately held asset that won't be divided should you divorce.

→ **If you're already married,** consult a family attorney about a postnuptial agreement, as well as buy-sell agreements (which set terms of business ownership transfer in advance) and shareholder agreements (which can set limits on the ownership rights of a founder's ex-spouse).[10]

We have spoken with a lot of founders whose marriages don't survive the launch and running of a business. However, a personal split doesn't always mean the end of a productive business relationship.

In 2017, I profiled Wana Brands, one of the most successful and high-profile makers of legal marijuana edibles. Co-owners Nancy and John Whiteman were married with two kids, working more traditional jobs in marketing and urban planning, respectively. When an acquaintance started working on a marijuana-infused soda business, the Whitemans were intrigued and decided to establish their own edibles company. Yet while the couple was setting up a new professional partnership, they were ending their personal one:

"Starting a business when we did, given where our marriage was at the time, was a brave act, many people thought," Nancy says, choosing her words carefully. "But there was the fun factor. We're both motivated by trying new things, and we thought, 'This would be so cool. Why not just try it?'"

She and John divorced in 2011, but found their footing as business partners. John would oversee Wana's operations and logistics, while Nancy would handle sales, finance, marketing, and business development, and be the public face of the company.[11]

Boulder, Colorado–based Wana Brands ended 2016 as the best-selling purveyor of marijuana-infused edibles in Colorado, according to industry data firm BDS Analytics.[12]

Figuring out how to involve your partner in your business can work out in many different ways, as long as you're willing to have the tough conversations. Starting a business involves lots of these conversations, such as the next section's topic.

ASKING FRIENDS OR FAMILY FOR MONEY

In 1992, Daymond John's one-year-old clothing company, FUBU, had scored what initially felt like a major victory. John had returned from FUBU's first display at a major retail trade show in Las Vegas, where the company had secured $300,000 in preorders. But there was a problem: John didn't have the cash necessary to get those orders to customers.

He tried to apply for a loan, but having never applied for one before, he didn't understand how to fill out the paperwork. After being rejected by twenty-seven banks, John realized he needed to come up with another solution—quickly.

He turned to his mom, who came up with the cash by mortgaging the family's house (where FUBU also manufactured its clothes) for $100,000.

That maternal leap of faith paid off for John: FUBU went on to generate more than $350 million in annual revenue by 1998, a success that helped land its founder a role as a judge on ABC's *Shark Tank*.[13]

Whether it's asking a parent to take out a mortgage, or drumming up funding for the more common "friends and family round," you'll probably wind up asking your loved ones for money to help your business. What promises should you make, and how should you protect both your business and your closest relationships?

Oren Bloostein, founder of New York coffee-shop chain Oren's Daily Roast, started that company with $30,000 of his own savings, $50,000 from his parents, and a bank loan for $25,000, which his parents also guaranteed. As he told *Inc.*'s Nicole Carter:

"I started the company in 1986, but it took almost a decade before I could borrow using assets from the business. The first eight years of expansion, which included six more stores and a factory, the loans were all guaranteed by my parents' assets," says Bloostein. "But the lines were clear. My parents weren't part owners, but my dad and I would have regular meetings, at which I would present him the numbers, projections, revenue, and everything."

His savvy approach helped his company become what it is today—a nearly $10 million business with nine locations in Manhattan. The moral of the story? Mom and Dad can be a great source of financing, but there's a right way (and a very wrong way) to approach that initial conversation about money.[14]

When asking your parents for money, much of what experts advise is comparable to the advice for communicating with your spouse:

→ **Make sure your parents' finances can afford to support your business** and that your request won't jeopardize their retirement or current standard of living.

→ **Approach them with a fully written, and fully vetted, business plan.** (Another good reason to write one!)

→ **Set a regular schedule for meetings** to update your parents on the business, and set the terms up front. "It doesn't have to be a daily conversation," Wayne Rivers, Family Business Institute president, told Carter. "Set up quarterly, or semiannual meetings where you will share the status of your business. Just something to give everyone a structure."[15]

→ **Write a promissory note** outlining the terms of the loan.

→ **If you have siblings, consider how they might react** to hearing that you've asked your parents for a lot of money. Communicate with them up front, and consider bringing them into the conversation with your parents.

→ **Financially protect your loved ones** when asking them for money. When pitching friends and family, Cadoux Hirshberg advises: "Be confident but also lay out the worst-case scenario: 'I don't know when you are going to get this back. You may lose it all. I may need you to up the ante in order to prevent dilution.'"[16]

She recommends drawing up shareholder agreements with no ambiguity, and refusing any offers to dip into college or retirement funds. "Don't take advantage of their eagerness to help," Cadoux Hirshberg says. "Your investors' hope is that this launch will be an exciting and profitable ride. Your role is to be the sober designated driver and bring everyone home safely."

→ **Financially protect yourself** when asking loved ones for money. "Many company founders are so grateful for the support and confidence being shown in them that they willingly agree to any terms their 'F&F' funders suggest," as Inc.com's Minda Zetlin reports.[17] She spoke with Alicia Navarro, cofounder of affiliate marketing company Skimlinks, who started her company with "friends and family" investments. Navarro's advice includes the following:

→ **Be clear about what your investors are getting** in exchange for their money. Navarro recommends offering friends and family a convertible note with a discount on conversion during your priced seed round—meaning you'll be getting a loan that will convert into stock in your company, usually when you raise your next round of funding.

→ **Try to keep legal costs down.** This depends on how much you trust your family members, and vice versa, but Navarro recommends trying to keep lawyers out of it if you're offering convertible notes instead of stock. You can consult publicly available templates for contracts or go more basic. "A simple email with bullet points on how their investment will become equity is fine, as long as your word means enough to them," she told Zetlin.

→ **Don't give up control.** In Chapter 4, we'll get into some of what traditional investors want you to give up for their money. But it's not worth giving up any control at this early stage, and presumably for a small fraction of the money you may someday want to raise. If your friends and family are asking for any venture-capital-type concessions, such as board seats or anti-dilution provisions, it's better to walk away.

If asking loved ones for money is complicated, going into business together can be even more so. On the one hand, you already know and trust your friend or spouse or sibling and will start the business with knowledge of your partner's strengths and weaknesses. On the other hand, many a personal relationship has been ruined by a sour business deal.

STARTING A BUSINESS TOGETHER

Bill Mackey was an original investor in Whole Foods, a long-time board member, and a mentor to his son [Whole Foods co-founder John Mackey]. But after Whole Foods went public in 1992, and kicked off an era of rapid expansion, the two found themselves embroiled in a classic go-slow-or-grow debate.

"I wanted to build the company," [John] Mackey says. "We were constantly arguing about whether we should do this store, whether we should make this acquisition. I just found him way too conservative."

In 1994, as he was turning forty, Mackey asked his father to resign. "The hardest thing I've ever done," Mackey says. "I had to overcome a lot of fear, because I was dependent on my dad, emotionally and intellectually. I knew it hurt him a lot—he felt rejected—so I felt guilty. It was a painful decision, and that pain lasted a while."

Mackey's father assented. One year later, he forgave his son.[18]

Whether with siblings, close friends, or spouses, if you're going to finance and operate a startup together, you should have some initial conversations:

→ **Discuss who does what,** and how to reconcile any overlapping responsibilities.

→ **Figure out who's putting up what money,** and how you'll split equity in the company.

→ **And, ideally, set ground rules** for when to keep the business out of your personal relationship. Baked by Melissa's founding siblings, Melissa Ben-Ishay and Brian Bushell, didn't set ground rules ahead of time, but "we probably should have," Ben-Ishay told me. "We're an incredible team, but it wasn't easy," she admitted. "If you disagree with him, and if you're in a conference room filled with people, maybe that's not so appreciated. I've realized that I just need to let things happen. And then we do our best to keep family time separate."[19]

You may want to declare one room of your apartment, or one time of day, or one weekly dinner, a no-work zone. Or you may not! Ultimately, the way you negotiate your cofounder relationship will be similar to how you negotiate any other close relationship: If you can't communicate early and often, it probably won't work.

When it does work out, it can really work out! Some couples who have started successful businesses together include Carley Roney and David Liu of The Knot; Marla Malcolm Beck and Barry Beck of Bluemercury; Robert L. and Sheila Johnson of BET (who ultimately divorced, but who also sold their company for $2.3 billion in stock); Matthew Malin and Andrew Goetz of Malin+Goetz;

Rita Sodi and Jody Williams of multiple successful Manhattan restaurants; and countless other pairs.

Malin and Goetz, for example, met at a bar more than two decades ago, and in 2004 founded their New York–based, high-end beauty company.

"Physically, emotionally, intellectually, we're pretty different people," Malin told *Inc.*'s Sheila Marikar. "Even our mindsets about business models: Andrew's free-spirited ideas about entrepreneurialism and my background of not taking big risks and being with a big company—I was the head of global sales at Kiehl's—it's the tension of being opposites and approaching things from different directions that has given us strength."[20] To which Goetz replied:

We have our Sid-and-Nancy moments. How do you derive the positive things about being opposites and living and working together and assuage the negative things? It's a constant battle.

But we've sort of figured out the formula, and the formula has changed. At the beginning, one great advantage we had was talking about work after hours. Then we bought a little farmhouse in upstate New York, and that's become our salvation.

Matthew will drive up Friday morning and I'll take the train up that evening so we have a day apart, which is healthy. Otherwise, it becomes all-encompassing.[21]

By early 2017, Malin+Goetz was opening its ninth retail location, and was selling its bath and beauty products in six hundred other retail outlets.

Family-founded businesses can be trickier. There's often a succession problem, even if you and your sibling or parent cofounders manage to get along: Most family businesses don't survive the

third generation. However, some family-owned businesses spec-
tacularly defy the odds—particularly if they figure out a way to
bring in nonfamily leadership, as I found when I looked into the
beloved East Coast convenience store that is Wawa.

Founded in 1964 by Grahame Wood, as the latest iteration of
a multi-business Philadelphia dynasty that dates back to 1682,
the onetime roadside dairy store "has weathered fifty-four years
of family in-fighting, recessions, and several failed expansion at-
tempts," I wrote:[22]

[Dick] Wood [Grahame's cousin and the company's second
CEO] kept Wawa private, but also started handing it off to
non-family leaders more than a decade ago, betting the best
way to ensure Wawa's future was to separate it from its founding family. His wager paid off. Wawa is still aggressively growing: It now has almost 800 locations—none franchised—and
30,000 employees in six states (plus Washington, DC). . . .

Like Wegmans or In-N-Out, Wawa is usually described as
a cult brand, a regional player—a mid-Atlantic specialist con-
fined to a narrow niche. That niche, though, is huge. The company claims $10 billion in annual revenue. (Wawa also says
it's profitable, though it won't discuss specifics or how much
revenue comes from gas sales.) Top dog in the $550 billion US
convenience store industry is 7-Eleven, which took in $29 bil-
lion in US revenue in 2017. But Wawa is now eyeing new competitors: quick-service and fast-casual chains like Dunkin'
Donuts or even Chipotle, which sells nearly $4.5 billion in
burrito bowls and guacamole annually.[23]

Wawa named its first nonfamily CEO in 2005, and is now 41 percent owned by its employees. Dick Wood explained both decisions

to me: "We decided a long time ago that what was important to the family was 'What's the value of a share of stock, and what's my dividend?'" he says. "The family is very happy to have somebody running the business who wants to grow the business."[24]

Which brings us to the next hard conversation: When might it be time to relinquish some of your business in exchange for a whole lot of money? Turn the page to read about everything venture capital.

LOOKING FOR OUTSIDE INVESTORS

" Make money before you start asking for it. The best way to validate your market is to get customers."[1]

ANGELA BENTON, founder and CEO of NewME Accelerator, which focuses on women- and minority-owned startups

" I always think that a business is a much better thing when I don't have to listen to anybody else, particularly when they're wagging their wallet at me. But if your business is going to fail—which would have happened at Cisco if we hadn't taken the money—you have to choose the devil you want to work with."[2]

SANDY LERNER, cofounder of Cisco, founder of Urban Decay and Ayrshire Farm

IT'S TIME. YOU'RE READY. You've bootstrapped your business as far as it will go, or you've got a brilliant idea that's tremendously expensive to finance, or you want to get to market as quickly as possible. You've watched every episode of *Shark Tank* and every episode of *Silicon Valley*, and you practice your pitch every day in the shower. You're ready to look for outside investors.

Seeking outside money is a daunting, grinding, tedious process. It can go horribly wrong. But raising money can also go tremendously well if you do your homework, network like crazy, and get lucky.

In this chapter, we'll walk you through most of the major sources of outside money you may want to seek for your business, including early-stage accelerators, the glamorous world of venture capital (VC), and the private-equity firms focused on more established businesses. We'll discuss some of the fundamental problems with the VC system and offer tips for how to get around them. And we'll give you a guide on how to negotiate a term sheet with investors, if you reach that stage.

Which means it's time for a reminder: Have you written your business plan yet? If not, turn back to Chapter 2 and do so.

Let's start with one of the first early options when you're considering a search for outside money.

SHOULD YOU CONSIDER AN INCUBATOR OR AN ACCELERATOR?

Techstars. Y Combinator. 500 Startups. As their names suggest, incubators and accelerators can provide jump-starts to young businesses, or nascent business ideas. They vary widely, but at their best can seem like a mashup of business school and a Silicon Valley boot camp.

Incubators and accelerators have some differences, though both tend to offer some sort of training or classes; access to experts and mentors; and, it is hoped, productive networking.

"*Incubators* tend to be longer (one to five years), and they don't frequently offer funding," *Inc.*'s Robin D. Schatz explains. "*Accelerators*, by contrast, offer funding in exchange for equity, tend to have short programs . . . and seek to ready startups for seed funding."[3]

Some incubators and accelerators focus on particular types of businesses, or on founders with specific backgrounds, such as those the traditional VC system underserves.

For instance, in 2011, serial entrepreneur Angela Benton launched NewME in San Francisco to focus on supporting minority and women founders. Within four years, her accelerator had worked with about three hundred startups worldwide, backing them with about $17 million collectively—especially after Benton switched from a twelve-week course to a one-week course, allowing her to work with more than sixteen entrepreneurs annually.[4]

"I saw all of this demand that really wasn't being served," she told *Inc.*'s 2015 Women's Summit. "I felt kind of stuck."[5]

If you're in the early stages of working on your business, looking for an appropriate incubator or accelerator might be a good first step. But do your homework: More than one founder has taken time off of work, relocated his or her business, or given up a stake in it in exchange for what Efrem Weiss, CEO of social-media site YouGift, experienced in 2012, as Schatz reports:

> Sadly, the experience turned into a decelerator. Mentoring sessions were group chats over Skype in a crowded room. The office's couches looked as if they were out of *Animal House*. Weiss pulled his team out two weeks later, negotiated the return of his equity, and slunk back to the city. He shut down the business in March 2013. He says YouGift might have survived if he had chosen his program more wisely.[6]

He and other alumni of incubators and accelerators suggest talking to others who have gone through the program you're considering, to ask if they would recommend it and to determine if the atmosphere fits the experience you want.

You could also consult the Seed Accelerator Rankings,[7] compiled by a team of professors from Rice University, University of Richmond, and Massachusetts Institute of Technology.[8] Their 2017 rankings put AngelPad and Y Combinator in the "platinum plus" highest tier, slightly above Alchemist, Amplify.LA, Chicago New Venture Challenge, MuckerLab, StartX, and Techstars.[9]

Before signing up for an accelerator or an incubator, you also should try to ensure that the program's mentors and managing directors have the expertise and specific connections your business needs, assess your willingness (and ability) to relocate to attend a program, and, of course, vet the program's financial and legal terms to ensure that you're willing to give up the equity requested—and that you can get it back if anything goes wrong.

Which is good advice, no matter what type of outside investor you're seeking. Let's review some of the others.

A GUIDE TO INVESTOR TYPES

Angel or seed. Wealthy individuals investing their own money, or accelerators.[10] They typically invest in very early-stage companies.

Venture capital (VC). Professional firms investing money they've raised from "limited partners," meaning banks, pension funds, and other big institutional investors. They invest in start-ups and companies with high-growth potential, such as younger businesses, generally take a minority stake, and can range from very passive to active.

Private equity (PE). Professional firms typically investing in older or more-established businesses, often using debt. PE investors tend to take a majority stake or seek a full buyout. They can help you expand rapidly, but they also often seek operational control of your company (meaning they'll want to replace you or at least call the shots).

"There comes a time when you need cash to grow—for new equipment, more inventory, and other resources to meet increased customer demand—and private equity has some of the deepest pockets," as *Inc.*'s Graham Winfrey asserts. "Still, private equity isn't for everyone, especially if your goal is to build a long-term independent business; most significant investments lead to an eventual outright sale (or public offering)."[11]

We'll discuss sales and IPOs (initial public offerings) in Chapter 5, regarding exit strategies.

Corporate investors. They look and sound and probably even dress like VCs, but they're from Citigroup. Or JetBlue. Or Campbell Soup. Big companies are setting up venture arms and investing in startups, and they have some unique attractions and drawbacks, as *Inc.*'s Alix Stuart reports:

> Big-company investors rarely offer huge sums but can give you advantages that traditional venture investors can't, says Evangelos Simoudis, a traditional VC who advises corporations on how to invest in, incubate, or acquire startups. For one, they are often customers of the startups they fund, or have some other type of actual or potential business relationship. That means industry expertise, proprietary technology, and access to networks that can juice your firm's growth. Such backing is also a credibility boost. For Getable, it's "proving to be much more valuable than just getting money," says [Getable founder Tim] Hyer.[12]

Not to mention that "corporate investors may be nicer," Stuart adds. "Kathy Leake, cofounder, CEO, and chairwoman of Qualia, which has gotten more than $16 million in venture funding, says her Verizon Ventures investors are 'less aggressive' than typical VCs, in part because they don't have limited partners to satisfy."[13]

Taking corporate investment may also lead to an eventual sale to the big company, although not always, as you'll read in Chapter 5.

Crowdfunding, equity- or rewards-based. Online fundraising for a specific product or project, or for your company overall, in exchange for either physical "rewards" (T-shirts, event tickets, one of the products) or, in some cases, for equity in your company. More traditional crowdfunding doesn't technically involve investment—you're not giving away pieces of your company—but it can put you on the hook to fulfill a lot of customer orders quickly. The crowdfunding platforms will also take a cut of whatever you raise, plus credit card processing charges—meaning you'll likely lose 8 percent or more to fees.[14]

"Kickstarter and Indiegogo are world-class inventions that changed the nature of funding for startups. But don't use such platforms prematurely. If you're trying to crowdfund your initial idea, that almost guarantees you are working on the wrong thing," Steve Blank, the Silicon Valley serial entrepreneur and Stanford adjunct professor whose customer-development methodology launched the Lean Startup movement, told *Inc.*'s Leigh Buchanan and Sheila Marikar. "The minute you commit to Kickstarter, if you get funded, you are entering two years of indentured servitude until you deliver that product."[15]

Equity crowdfunding, legalized by the JOBS Act (the Jumpstart Our Business Startups Act, signed into law in 2012, intended to encourage funding of small businesses), allows you to sell small pieces of your company to people who are not "accredited investors" (meaning people with more than $200,000 in annual income or a net worth of more than $1 million). It's a new and fairly complicated way of raising money, so consult a lawyer and regulatory expert before taking it on.

Initial coin offerings. Just don't. Enough said.

Now that you've identified the sort of money you want to go after, it's time to consider your courtship strategy.

THE END IS NOT NECESSARILY THE END

“ Raising money was a year and a half of my life, and I loved every minute of it. Boy, was it grinding and difficult. At the end of it, my husband was like, 'Does this mean I get my wife back?' because you're going to war. You're going to the mattresses a little bit, and not necessarily in a negative way. It doesn't have to be argumentative. You can't do a good deal with bad people, and you can't do a bad deal with good people. I often use that as my compass.”[16]

—
CHRISTINA TOSI, founder and CEO of Milk Bar

“Picking an investor is like getting married.” Almost every startup founder says that, and with good reason: You're committing to people who now have a financial stake in your company—and while they wouldn't invest if they didn't believe in you, you'll also have to figure out if these are the people you want to spend the rest of your business life, well, in bed with.

The consequences of choosing poorly can be shattering. Sandy Lerner, a tireless serial entrepreneur, was a computer scientist at Stanford University when she and her then husband, Leonard Bosack, cofounded the company that became networking giant Cisco Systems. When their company needed money, they picked the wrong investor, as Lerner told *Inc.*'s Jeremy Quittner:

After funding the company for three years by mortgaging everything we owned and putting everything on credit cards, we made an absolutely bozo no-no.

We decided to take money from a VC, Don Valentine. He got 30-odd percent of the company for $2.6 million. Len and I were very naive. We used Don's lawyer and agreed to a four-year vesting agreement. We would get 90 percent of the founder's stock after four years. But we didn't get an employment contract.

When I was fired, it was devastating. I spent years crawling out from that. I did not understand an investor could be an adversary. My family had a small business. I always thought that if someone invested in your business, that meant he or she believed in it. I assumed our investor supported us, because his money was tied up in our success. I did not realize he had decoupled the success of the company from that of the founders.

I don't believe all VCs are adversarial, but the first thing I tell everyone is: Get your own lawyer.[17]

Lerner was ousted from Cisco in 1990, shortly after the company went public. She rebounded impressively, going on to start cosmetics company Urban Decay, which sold to L'Oreal for an estimated $350 million. Then she wrote a sequel to *Pride and Prejudice* and turned her attention to organic farming. Today Lerner's food empire includes her 800-acre Ayrshire Farm, plus restaurant and retail offshoots.[18]

Hardware entrepreneur Danielle Applestone had a similarly bad experience. After growing up in rural Arkansas, Applestone made her way to Massachusetts Institute of Technology, earned a Ph.D. in material science, and created a cutting-edge, computer-controlled desktop milling machine called the Othermill, an invention that experts believe has the potential to be more significant than consumer 3-D printers. Through crowdfunding and angel and venture investors, Applestone raised $6.5 million for her company, Other Machine, now known as Bantam Tools.

When her investors ran out of patience, Applestone's company almost shut down. As *Inc.*'s Kimberly Weisul reports:

> By 2017, she'd been shipping product for three years and had reached breakeven, no small feat for a hardware startup. But at a board meeting that February, her investors told her it wasn't enough. They wanted to see the kind of growth trajectory that would bring dramatic returns, and they didn't think Applestone was on that path. She needed to do something radically different, they told her, or it would be time to sell. Suddenly, the funding bargain she'd made became very clear to her: "We couldn't keep doing what we were doing because we'd taken venture capital."[19]

She found a new life for her company by lining up a like-minded buyer—MakerBot cofounder and former CEO Bre Pettis—who's now working with Applestone to expand her business.

But many founders have much happier stories about their investors. Pastry chef and *MasterChef* judge Christina Tosi, for example, started her Milk Bar bakery with seed funding from her then employer, Momofuku founder David Chang. Cue scrambling:

> Dave knew I wanted to open up a bakery, and one day this tenant next to one of his restaurants was leaving. He said, "This is your love. I'll help you get the space. Just go and do it."
>
> Where my normal head would go into overplanning and weighing all my options, I didn't have time for that. It wasn't about having a P&L. It was just: I have forty-five days to make this happen. I didn't have time to worry about, "What if people

don't come, or what if people think the name Compost Cookie is a crazy, horrid thing to name a cookie?" I didn't have time for self-doubt.

I had a moment on opening morning—at like 4:00 or 5:00 a.m.—baking cookies with the three people who were crazy enough to follow me down this path. Then we opened the door, and there was a line around the corner, down the block. It was like a cannon ball and we were off.[20]

Tosi told me that she repaid Chang's seed investment and then avoided seeking investor money for years. "We were profitable, and at first I would be really strategic about the money we made: 'OK. If I do this project, we can buy a delivery van. If I write a cookbook, we can open three stores,'" she told me. "That was my growth strategy in part because I'm stubborn, and in part because plenty of people say, 'Don't take money unless you need it. You don't want to give away a piece of your business if you don't need to.'"[21]

But Tosi soon realized that she wanted to expand faster than bootstrapping would permit—and she needed to be able to finance more risk-taking in her business. Which set off a year and a half of searching for the right investor. By late 2017, Milk Bar had closed a reported eight-figure funding round from RSE Ventures, money that Milk Bar will use to expand locations, e-commerce operations, and product lines.

If, like Tosi, you realize you're ready to seek funding, how do you find the perfect money mate, and how do you know they're the right match?

Tosi went looking for "good people." When he was still at MakerBot, Bre Pettis told us, "Our rule was, we wouldn't accept money from anybody we didn't want to have dinner with."[22]

You can substitute "dinner" for bike rides or beers or barre classes, or any other forum for figuring out your compatibility with your potential investors. Like dating, you'll need some way to figure out whether you want to commit to this person. However, you need to find them first.

THE SEARCH

As with many other parts of your career, whom you know counts. Only about 10 percent of VC deals resulted from cold calls by startup founders, according to a comprehensive April 2017 working paper by researchers at Harvard, Stanford, and the University of Chicago.[23] Most VC deals originated from the investor's "professional network" (31 percent) or "self-generated" research (28 percent).

Flavored-water entrepreneur Jody Levy, for example, lined up an investment from music superstar Beyoncé Knowles with a seeming cold call that also involved lots of behind-the-scenes networking. When Beyoncé's "Drunk in Love" single mentioned that the singer had been "drinking watermelon," Levy sent the singer's team a couple cases of the cold-pressed watermelon juice that her company, World Waters, had been working to get on the Whole Foods shelves.

It wasn't an entirely unsolicited drinks package. Levy told *Inc.*'s Christine Lagorio-Chafkin that, before she sent the samples, a friend had made an introduction to Beyoncé's Parkwood Entertainment Group.[24] And both kinds of hustle paid off: In 2016, Beyoncé invested an undisclosed amount in Levy's company.[25]

As that story demonstrates, lining up the right investor for your business could take months, or even years.

Polina Raygorodskaya, cofounder and CEO of transportation website Wanderu, told me that one of the biggest money mistakes she made with her business was starting to raise money at the wrong time of year—specifically, during summer vacation season.

"Typically, when you go and fundraise, you want to give yourself at least six months runway in the bank, because fundraising always takes a lot longer than you think it's going to take. I knew that, so I gave myself six months," Raygorodskaya told me during a panel discussion at *Inc.*'s Women's Summit in 2017.[26]

"The problem was that I started raising money in May. So, all of the partners end up going on vacation in the summer, and time kills all deals," she added. "I learned very quickly, after almost running out of money, that I should have raised earlier—and given myself nine months of runway."[27]

Raygorodskaya confirmed the investment in the nick of time, *Inc.*'s Zoe Henry reports: "In November 2014, after months of trying to pull together $5.6 million in funding—and considering salary cuts—Raygorodskaya was able to lock in the investment, giving her time and teaching her a formative lesson: prioritize generating a profit."[28]

If you do attract VC interest, "you have to kiss a lot of frogs," warns Steve Kaplan, a professor of entrepreneurship and finance at the University of Chicago's Booth School of Business, and one of four coauthors of the working paper investigating what interests venture capitalists.[29]

Then there's the unfair part, especially if you're looking specifically for venture capital. According to a recent study by the Boston Consulting Group and MassChallenge, a network of startup accelerators, businesses founded or cofounded by women are granted less than half of the average investment in male-founded businesses—$935,000 versus $2.1 million. That funding gap persists even though, according to the same study, women-founded businesses bring in $730,000 in cumulative revenue over a five-year period—more than the $662,000 made by male-founded businesses.[30]

"Dollar-for-investment-dollar, the differences are even more stark: For every dollar raised, women-run startups generated 78 cents in revenue, compared to 31 cents for men," *Inc.*'s Kimberly Weisul reports. "By that measure, if investors had put the same amount of capital into women-run companies as they did into the ones run by guys, they would have helped generate an additional $85 million in revenue."[31]

This isn't a one-off finding. Women own a third of businesses in the United States, but get a laughably small percentage of venture money. Weisul's 2016 article surveys the grim landscape:

While women start companies at twice the rate of men, female-founded companies get only 13 percent of the total angel financing available. According to a study by First Round Capital, companies with a woman on the founding team outperform their all-male peers by 63 percent. But when it comes to venture capital—often the speediest route to building a fast-growth company—women simply aren't getting funded. Female CEOs get only 2.7 percent of all venture funding, while women of color get virtually none: 0.2 percent. . . .

In 1999, the portion of venture capital deals that went to a startup with a woman on the executive team was just 5 percent. It's taken nearly twenty years to increase that amount to 18 percent. It's no better when you look at the profession itself. In 1999, 10 percent of venture capitalists were women; today, their number has sunk to just 6 percent.[32]

Part of this funding gap results from ignorance or disinterest. VCs are overwhelmingly male, meaning that women pitching better bras, or breast pumps, or clothing-in-a-box often meet blank stares across the table.

"Ninety percent of the time, you're pitching mostly to men," Heidi Zak, cofounder of bra startup ThirdLove, told *Inc.*'s Liz Welch:

> In pitches, [ThirdLove designer Ra'el] Cohen would unveil the startup's bra prototypes, but more often than not, the discussions would devolve into Mad Men clichés—male VCs calling in their female assistants and junior-level associates to evaluate the startup's worthiness. After meeting with one top Silicon Valley firm, [cofounder Dave] Spector says a male partner told them he didn't want to invest "because 'we invest only in markets we understand.'"[33]

"Your business is on fire, your team is great, but I just don't feel passionate about women's apparel," is how Katrina Lake, cofounder and CEO of styling service Stitch Fix, described some VC reactions to her company to *Inc.*'s Jeff Bercovici. "My hope is we can show venture capitalists that companies are successful even though they may not be the passion they have."[34]

Of course, part of the reason for the funding gap is outright bias, or worse, as Lake herself discovered. She was among the founders who were sexually harassed by Justin Caldbeck, a prominent venture capitalist and a onetime observer to Stitch Fix's board.

Caldbeck lost his roles at Binary Capital, the venture firm he cofounded, and at Stitch Fix, while Lake led her company to raise $120 million in a 2017 IPO. Less than a year later, Lake is overseeing a profitable company with a $4.35 billion market cap.

Unfortunately, Lake is hardly alone in having to overcome harassment and bias in her fundraising efforts. As many a #MeToo revelation has highlighted in the past year, "women seeking financing face many less measurable challenges," *Inc.*'s Helaine Olen writes, "including sexist treatment ranging from the merely condescending to out-and-out harassment."[35]

New investment groups are being formed with the express purpose of investing in women and minorities—and they're often run by women. Not to mention that specialist accelerators can build relationships with investors. Golden Seeds, Susan Lyne's BBG, and Female Founders Fund are just a few of these new groups. Additionally, Backstage Capital founder Arlan Hamilton and Sundial Brands cofounder Richelieu Dennis have both announced funds that will invest in black women entrepreneurs.[36]

Hamilton, a onetime music-industry production coordinator, knows what it's like to struggle for money to fund her dream. She'd quit her job to chase down investors and try to build a different kind of VC fund, one that would invest in female, minority, and LGBTQ entrepreneurs. In spite of her inclusivity aspirations, by September 2015 Hamilton was struggling and homeless, as *Inc.*'s Sal Rodriguez reports:

> Hamilton had met with every investor she could track down and cold-called everyone in tech she could think of. No one had written her a check. Why would they? Hamilton, an African American lesbian, was a Silicon Valley outsider. She had

no track record as a venture capitalist. And she wanted to invest in a segment of founders with little proven success.

She'd spent everything to bootstrap her mission. For months, she'd been homeless, sleeping on couches, in motels, out of cars, at airports. As a weary Hamilton sat, contemplating her next move, her phone buzzed.

"I'm in," read the text from Susan Kimberlin, a tech veteran who made a name for herself at Salesforce and PayPal. Kimberlin was ready to bet on Hamilton to bring more diversity to tech—and her check was the lifeline Hamilton needed to get Backstage Capital up and running.

Hamilton sat there in silence, lost in thought, letting the moment sink in. "I made it," she thought to herself before standing up to do a moonwalk and a little twirl. Then immediately, she went back to work, calling the startups she'd been wanting to invest in for months. She picked up her bags and started walking.

"I never had to be homeless again after that," she says.[37]

Three years later, Hamilton's Backstage Capital had made seed-stage investments in eighty companies, all of which have one founder who is a woman, a person of color, or LGTBQ. She's also launching a $36 million fund that invests only in black female founders.[38]

In 2001, Sheila Lirio Marcelo was working in marketing for a tech company and had recently given birth to her second son. Her parents were visiting from the Philippines to help with childcare when her father had a heart attack and wound up requiring around-the-clock medical care—meaning that Marcelo and her husband had to find someone to take care of both her father and her sons.

Thus was hatched the idea for online caretaker marketplace Care.com, which Marcelo launched in 2006. Before taking her company public in 2014, she raised more than $110 million in venture funding—even if she did sometimes get mistaken by investors as the company's assistant, not the CEO. As Marcelo told *Inc.*'s Diana Ransom:

> During our IPO road show, we flew into this private airport. I went straight for the coffeepot. Our CTO, a male, shook hands. Our CFO, a male, shook hands. When I got there, I offered people coffee. They thought I was the assistant. That happens. So, my goal is to change people's unconscious bias. By putting them on the spot in a polite, respectful way, it makes them say, "Huh, the next time I look at a woman, I'm not going to assume she's the assistant.". . .
>
> Women need to feel very confident in their numbers, and they need to feel solid about their business plans. If you need to practice your pitches with friends, you should. Also, if you're not fully confident about the numbers, find cofounders who are.[39]

As one of the few women tech founders in recent years to take a company public, Marcelo frequently gets asked for her advice on the fundraising process. According to *Inc.*'s Kimberly Weisul, the Care.com founder advises not relying too much on funds that are owned by or targeted toward women. But Marcelo also "says it's a good idea to make a point to at least network with female venture backers, for two reasons," according to Weisul:

> First is that you just want to run your idea by as many people as possible, and women may very well have a different

perspective on it than men. Second is that women venture capitalists, she says, "are always wanting to support female entrepreneurs and will recommend angel investors."[40]

Meanwhile, crowdfunding sites like Kickstarter and Indiegogo have proven to be places where women have a better chance of getting financing. As we've discussed, however, crowdfunding isn't for everyone. Alicia Robb, a senior fellow at the Ewing Marion Kauffman Foundation, wrote in *Inc.*:

Women make up 44 percent of investors on Kickstarter, according to research by Kauffman and the Hebrew University of Jerusalem. That's a better balance than the VC or angel investor community can lay claim to. It also demonstrates a ready audience for products made by women, a number of which are specifically targeted at women. For example, Willa founder Christy Prunier raised $1 million on CircleUp in 2012 to fund her natural skincare company, which she started with (and named after) her then twelve-year-old daughter.[41]

For all entrepreneurs, some ways you can find the right person to pitch include the following:

→ **Attend pitch contests, meetups, and other events** in your industry.

→ **Research investors** who specialize in your company type. For instance, if you run a cloud-software startup, don't try to meet with VCs that have portfolios full of consumer goods companies.

→ **Work your networks, asking for warm introductions,** especially from any angel or seed investors in your company or people who have previously expressed interest in funding you.

Once you've set up a meeting, you still have a lot of homework to do.

THE PITCH

" Inevitably, they're going to ask questions you can't answer. If you're writing down the twentieth question to which you don't have an answer, that's a problem. You can say 'I'll get back to you,' but not more than five times."[42]

—

JESSICA ALBA, actor and cofounder of The Honest Company

" I wish we had done more research on it, because we went into it with a little bit of hubris and a lot of naivete. When you see company after company raising money, you get the outside-in perception—'It's not that difficult, if they can do it.' Which is not the case. We were two ex-McKinsey consultants, neither of us was technical, and we wanted to tackle insurance—every strike was against us. It was a very fruitless and frustrating few months."[43]

—

JENNIFER FITZGERALD, cofounder and CEO of Policygenius

Before you meet with someone you're going to ask for money, know your business plan inside and out. Know your numbers, know your company, and be prepared. (Aren't you glad you wrote your business plan?)

Also, do your homework on the people to whom you're pitching. If you can, talk to other entrepreneurs they've invested in. And, as Policygenius CEO Jennifer Fitzgerald learned to her chagrin, have experts look over your pitch deck.

Fitzgerald, a onetime international development worker, went to law school and then, in the middle of the recession, started working at McKinsey, consulting with giant insurance companies. She and her colleague Francois de Lame had an idea to build a more modern, online insurance brokerage, and decided to take a leave of absence to work on what would become Policygenius.

Then they started fundraising. It did not go well, Fitzgerald recounted to me recently: "If we got to the point where they did want to see our pitch deck, the early iterations were terrible," she recalled. "I think we may have shown the first pitch deck with footnotes ever. That went over like a lead balloon."[44]

Fitzgerald and her cofounder pitched hundreds of firms and realized they would have to raise their initial seed funding via friends and family rather than from VCs. They were trying to raise $1 million and fell short, scraping together $750,000.

Nevertheless, they persisted. Fitzgerald and de Lame used that $750,000 to build an initial product, got some early media attention, and went back into the fundraising trenches:

It took, oh gosh, five months to find a VC investor who believed in us. We really clicked. He got it. He actually had to advance us some of the cash, because we were a month away from running out of money and not making payroll.

After we got that first term sheet in, it got easier. Investing can be very much a herd mentality, so as soon as you have one institutional investor who will say, "I believe in this company, and I'm gonna lead the round," it's easy to round up other venture firms.[45]

Despite their early struggles, Fitzgerald and de Lame went on to raise $52 million in equity financing. Policygenius, based in New York, now has more than $10 million in annual revenue and 130 employees.

If you're starting your fundraising efforts, realize that you may need to be patient.

Mark Suster, a veteran entrepreneur and prominent VC at Upfront Ventures, told *Inc.*'s Jessica Bruder that he also recommends:

→ Come with questions to ask the VCs, so your pitch is a two-way conversation.

→ Be prepared to address any big, public problems—such as a cofounder departing or any bad press—but wait to bring up other big issues until the funding conversation is a bit further along.

→ Ask the VCs for referrals if it seems like their firm isn't quite the right fit.[46]

And, like dating, just because someone's interested in you doesn't mean he or she is good for you. Which brings us to . . .

THE PROPOSAL

Congratulations, someone wants to marry you! Should you say yes or no?

Sometimes you have to make these decisions on the fly, especially if you weren't out there seeking investment or a buyer. (It does happen.) Whether you've received an unsolicited bid, or you hooked a VC sooner than you were expecting, take these next steps:

→ **Schedule meetings** with any other suitors, to ensure you're getting the best deal, and not just settling for the first offer. "If someone has come to you, only very rarely is no one else interested," Brent Ridge, the cofounder of lifestyle company Beekman 1802, told *Inc.*'s Helaine Olen.[47]

→ **Make sure the offer aligns** with your short- and long-term goals for your company.

→ **Talk to a lawyer** with expertise in startup deals and, if things have reached this stage, have him or her review the term sheet.

NEGOTIATING THE TERM SHEET

As with any financial deal, when negotiating with investors, pay close attention to the paperwork details. You won't get everything you want—"It's not particularly negotiable," warns University of Chicago's Steve Kaplan[48]—but you should at least know what you're sacrificing, and what you're getting.

VCs tend to be more flexible on terms surrounding their right to invest in subsequent rounds, and their ability to get paid if the company liquidates, but are less flexible on valuation and control over the board of directors, according to research by Kaplan and his coauthors.

And you need to watch out for a few more things, as *Inc.*'s Annalyn Kurtz reports:

→ **Do you want to stay in control** of your company at all costs? Scrutinize terms that dictate *board seats, investor veto rights* (allowing investors to reject future financing offers), or *drag-along rights* (which may allow an investor to force the sale of a company).

→ **Do you want your company to grow,** even without you? Focus on terms concerning your startup's *valuation, options pool* (equity for your workers), and *liquidation preference* (who gets paid first if you fail).

→ **Look beyond the headline numbers,** like the investment and valuation sizes, to see how much control investors are asking for—and how much they get paid if your company gets sold. For example, a term sheet entitling investors to *nonparticipating preferred stock* means they will recoup their initial investment at a specified multiple, plus dividends. If the term sheet instead asks for *participating preferred stock*, your investors may be entitled to an even larger share when the company is sold. "It's only a one-word difference, and it could be a huge economic change," Stephanie Zeppa, a corporate and securities partner for San Francisco–based law firm Sheppard, Mullin, Richter & Hampton, told Kurtz.

→ **Consider using a Y Combinator SAFE Contract,** which allows an investor to make a cash investment that may convert to stock in a future equity financing round or merger (SAFE = "simple agreement for future equity"). These contracts include investor-friendly clauses like *pro rata rights* (the ability to participate in future funding rounds), but leave out more controversial board-seat privileges and veto rights.

→ **Be prepared to walk away** if you feel like you're being pressured into too many compromises. After all, if one investor finds your company attractive, odds are that others will, too.[49]

When you do find that perfect mate, it can be the start of a rewarding relationship. As Christina Tosi told me:

> I'm really, really, really happy with the decision that I made. One, to raise the money; two, to wait nine years to raise the money. I think that's an anomaly in this day and age. You typically raise money and then you go, and then you raise more money and then you go.
>
> I wanted to make sure I had a real business on my hands—not just a brand that people lusted after, with the dirty little secret that we didn't make money. Patience is a virtue.[50]

Speaking of patience—it's time to think about what you should do when you're ready to take some money out of your business, which is discussed in the next chapter about exit strategies.

EXIT
STRATEGIES

> " When you found a company, you feel a deep sense of responsibility for it. I'll care about Dell even after I'm dead."[1]

MICHAEL DELL in 2014

YOU MAY PLAN TO own your company until the day you die. But if you've taken any outside investments and your backers are ready to get repaid, or if you need a lot of money to expand, or if you get an offer you can't refuse, or if you just want to retire to a beach house somewhere, you'll have to think about your exit.

Which can mean a lot of things. Traditionally, "exiting" your company means selling it and walking away, or at least selling your stake in it to other owners. It could also mean taking it public—thus selling it to Wall Street investors—and having to walk away.

Today, "exiting" can also mean selling your company to a bigger company that wants to retain you as the head of what you created—or it can mean taking your company to the public markets but sticking around for the ride.

Or maybe even coming back. Michael Dell, for example, founded his eponymous technology company out of his dorm room in 1984. By 1990, he was a multimillionaire by age twenty-four, when *Inc.* named him entrepreneur of the year.

And he's stuck with his company through many a transition and multiple seeming exits: Since 1988, Dell has taken his company public, stepped down as CEO, returned as CEO three years later, taken Dell private again in 2013, and—as of this writing—announced plans to return his company to the public markets again.

"The point is, you can't keep doing the same thing and expect it to keep working," Dell told *Inc.*'s Tom Foster.[2] Dell was talking about products and company strategy, but the same sentiment apparently applies to corporate structure.

Dell's approach to the public-private divide reflects something we hear often from founders contemplating an IPO, who argue that going public is more of "a financing event" than a real exit.

"If you look at what going public enables, it's just the beginning of the next stage of the company," Jeff Lawson, cofounder and CEO of cloud-software company Twilio, told *Inc.*'s Will Yakowicz:

> If you think it's an exit, it can send the message that it's the end, and if you're an investor, you do not want to invest in a company that feels it is at the end. That's not the way an entrepreneur or a CEO or anybody involved should think about going public. I don't really understand the notion of exits, personally, because the point of building a company is to make it bigger and stronger every day, and fundraising and going public help you achieve the goal of creating a long-term, great company.[3]

Twilio raised $150 million in its 2016 IPO, and ended the following year with $399 million in revenue.

You might not share Lawson's attitude toward exits. But no matter how you feel about finding an off-ramp from your business, only you can decide the best path for you. In this chapter, we'll discuss the most common exit types and provide a guide about what you need to know for each.

IPOS VERSUS M&A

Both types of exits have advantages and drawbacks, and both require a lot of work to pull off successfully. IPOs tend to require even more work up front, and—if you're planning to remain in charge afterward—after the fact, as well.

Practically, you're much more likely to sell your company than take it public. There were more than 9,900 small-business sales in 2017, according to marketplace BizBuySell.com[4]—versus just 160 US IPO pricings that year, according to Renaissance Capital.[5]

(It's been a slow couple of years for initial public offerings, but even during the busier periods of the last couple of decades, the number of companies going public every year is in the hundreds, not the thousands.)[6]

Let's start with the sales process.

SELLING YOUR COMPANY

    " I made the decision ultimately for two reasons. One, I don't come from a particularly wealthy family, and so it would change my personal situation in a very meaningful way. And two, I'm a bit old school with my investments. It was the recession when we were acquired in 2009. I didn't want to risk it."[7]

AARON PATZER, founder and CEO of Mint.com, which he sold to Intuit for $170 million

" At first we were like, 'We're small, we'll handle it ourselves.' As you grow, you start to be open to other discussions."[8]

——

MARLA MALCOLM BECK, cofounder and CEO of Bluemercury, which she sold to Macy's in 2015 for $210 million

It's a good time to sell a business. In 2017, 9,919 small businesses changed hands, up 27 percent from 7,842 such deals the previous year, according to marketplace BizBuySell.com. The median sales price for small businesses rose to $227,880, while the median revenue of the firms for sale was $500,000.[9]

Founders sell their companies for all sorts of reasons. Some, like Bluemercury's Marla Malcolm Beck, find a buyer with more resources to expand their company. Some, like Mint.com's Aaron Patzer, see an opportunity for a good payday that will secure their futures.

Patzer started Mint.com after becoming frustrated by the amount of time it took him to organize his personal finances using traditional computer-based programs such as Quicken and Microsoft Money. He quit his day job, spent seven months building and designing Mint.com, and launched it to the public in September 2007.[10]

Two years later, Intuit bought Patzer's startup for $170 million. "I honestly didn't have an exit strategy," Patzer told *Inc.*'s David Whitford. "It took me four or five months before I made the decision to sell. We went back and forth."[11]

But the amount of money on offer during the recession convinced Patzer—who then had a much easier time raising money for his next startup, called Fountain: "With Mint, I had fifty nos before my first yes," Patzer told Whitford. "With Fountain, I simply told a couple of VCs what the idea was, and they offered me $4 million in financing with no effort whatsoever, with really good terms."[12]

Selling is a particularly common exit for small-business owners nearing the end of their careers, who count on selling their company to fund their retirement.

If that describes you, and you share ownership in the business, make sure you and your co-owners have a *buy-sell agreement* in place. As *Inc.*'s Kathy Kristof explains, these contracts will help you retire when you're ready, even if your co-owners aren't yet ready to sell. Buy-sell agreements are particularly important in larger partnership businesses, such as medical, law, or accounting firms. Kristof adds:

> A buy-sell agreement needs several components, including a formula for valuing privately held shares on the basis of verifiable metrics, which will vary by industry. Such a formula allows you to determine what your shares are likely to be worth. The buy-sell agreement should also list the conditions under which you may sell shares, to whom you may sell them, and how quickly or slowly such sales may take place.[13]

According to a 2018 MassMutual survey, only about 40 percent of business owners had such an agreement in place.[14] If you're part of the other 60 percent, set a date with your business partners and a lawyer to draw up the papers.

If you're the sole owner of your business, and hoping to sell it to fund your retirement, start planning several years ahead. Get your books in order, and be prepared to show several years' worth of sales figures, *Inc.*'s Jennifer Alsever reports: "'Ideally, your company should have at least one year of sustainable growth before going on the market,' says Mike Maak, president of

NorthEast Business Advisors in Rochester, Massachusetts. 'You could sweeten the deal by helping finance the sale and agreeing to stay on as a consultant.'"[15]

Bob House, president of BizBuySell.com, also suggests taking these steps to get your business ready to sell:[16]

→ **Have clean, presentable financial records.** And if you can show the business is still increasing in profitability, all the better.

→ **Get to know your potential buyer.** It will build trust, and ease the takeover for both of you, and for your employees.

→ **Create seamless processes and create incentives for key employees** to remain after you depart, thus assuring your buyer that the business will thrive even after you're gone.

→ **Spruce up the place.** "If you've been considering any renovations, new furniture purchases, or even just a fresh coat of paint, make sure it is all complete before any buyers step foot in the door," House writes on Inc.com.[17]

We don't necessarily advise this, but if you're the only owner of your company, sometimes you can afford to be more spontaneous with your sales negotiations.

Before she was a judge on *Shark Tank*, Barbara Corcoran spent nearly three decades building her real-estate brokerage into the profitable Corcoran Group. In 2001, she decided it was time to sell her business, and worked to attract the interest of real-estate giant NRT.

Corcoran was on vacation, in a ski resort's chairlift, when an NRT board member called her with an offer of $22 million to buy her company. She did some quick thinking and asked for $66 million instead.

"I figured I'd take a shot at it," Corcoran told *Inc.*'s Liz Welch. "Every time they came back, I stuck to it."[18]

NRT agreed to Corcoran's asking price, which was triple the opening bid.

SELLING—AND STAYING

" We can do more, faster, now that we're owned by Unilever—and now that I don't have to spend my time fundraising every year. But we operate completely independently. . . . [Dollar Shave Club is Dollar Shave Club] because of the decisions we have made in-house, and Unilever respects that."[19]

MICHAEL DUBIN, founder of Dollar Shave Club, which sold to Unilever for a reported $1 billion in 2016

" On a startup budget, you stretch and reach . . . and now we're like, 'Let's just go out and get the best.'"[20]

ALEXA VON TOBEL, founder of LearnVest, which sold to Northwestern Mutual in 2015 for a reported $250 million

Dollar Shave Club. Bluemercury. MyFitnessPal. These are just a few of the fast-growing startups that have been snapped up in recent years by big corporate overlords who wanted the startup founders, too.

This sort of corporate M&A is providing some founders a chance to stay with their companies, while getting the resources and reach of big corporate buyers. As *Inc.*'s Kimberly Weisul writes in a 2017 cover story about these internal entrepreneurs, or "disrupters in residence":

> In the past, when a big company bought a small one, the founder got a big payday, but had to accept giving up control of a business built on years of love and grueling work, and that the acquirer, once in control, might have a slightly different plan for its new toy. Cultures clashed, cherished employees left, and all the excitement that went into creating the merger vanished. Even worse was the "acquihire," in which a company got taken out primarily for its talent—without even a pretense of synergy.
>
> In the trend that's emerging, the founders of prominent startups are finding ways to sell their cake and have it too. They can run their brands on their own terms inside larger corporations while at the same time providing spark and nimbleness to the parent company. "We needed some sort of outside catalyst to get our digital effort going at the speed I wanted it to," says John Schlifske, CEO of Northwestern Mutual, which bought fintech startup LearnVest. "I didn't feel we had the right speed and agility." . . .
>
> Whether it's Northwestern Mutual jump-starting its online financial planning [with Alexa von Tobel's LearnVest], or Under Armour building a connected fitness initiative with a startup such as MyFitnessPal, this is how the smart twenty-first-century acquisition gets done. "At some point, established companies have to adopt some startup

thinking," says Alexander Chernev, a professor of marketing at the Kellogg School of Management. "It's not that startup thinking is the best thing ever. But it forces you to look at the world as a changing place."[21]

Of course, it matters to whom you sell your company. Mike Lee, cofounder of MyFitnessPal, told Weisul that he was uninterested in selling to a Google or an Apple, where "we would become one small piece in this giant machine." But after Under Armour founder and CEO Kevin Plank invited Lee to visit, and pitched him on a bigger strategy for "connected fitness," Lee started to see possibilities.

"At Under Armour, we knew we would matter," Lee recalled. "We would have the attention of the CEO, we would be a big part of the strategy, and we would make a difference."

He and his cofounder (and brother), Albert, agreed to sell My-FitnessPal to Under Armour for $475 million in February 2015. A year later, the fitness app had gone from 80 million users to "well over 100 million." (The Lee brothers did eventually leave Under Armour, in January 2018.)

Or there's Stacy Brown-Philpot, CEO of TaskRabbit, the gig economy service started by Leah Busque. Brown-Philpot, a former Google executive and one of most prominent black women in Silicon Valley, took over TaskRabbit in 2016 and sold it to Ikea a year later. "There's an obvious synergy between the two businesses," *Inc.*'s Sonya Mann explained at the time. "Consumers can buy furniture at Ikea, then hire someone from TaskRabbit to assemble the darn things."[22]

But, as Mann added, the deal also made sense for Ikea, given TaskRabbit's data trove on consumer habits and spending. "Ikea does extensive ethnographic research, examining potential customers' needs and behaviors, then shapes its products accordingly," she writes, adding that TaskRabbit "has a huge trove of data about how people live their domestic lives—especially affluent millennials, a demographic always coveted by big box retailers. TaskRabbit can help Ikea fill in the gaps. In a way, it's reminiscent of Unilever buying Dollar Shave Club in order to catch up to the age of the internet."[23]

Meanwhile, Brown-Philpot says that when she took over TaskRabbit, she was advised to make a list of the potential buyers she would even consider talking to. Ikea was on the list, she told the *New York Times*, because the retailer's values were aligned with TaskRabbit's.

"When we told our employees, everyone clapped because they were like, 'Oh, thank god. We're actually selling to a company that we admire and we respect,'" Brown-Philpot told the *Times*.[24] "That's when you know you've done the right thing."

Still, not every big corporate purchase of a startup goes well. Technology gets shut down, founders get shunted to the side, products get retooled. (Remember Vine, or Del.icio.us, or HopStop?)

"My one regret was agreeing to stay on for four years. I wound up leaving after a year," Jonathan Sposato, founder of software startup Phatbits, says of selling it to Google. "I underestimated what it would feel like to be a salaryman, no longer in control of my own destiny."[25]

That didn't stop Sposato from selling his next company, photo editing site Picnik, to Google—and facing some new challenges, as he told *Inc.*:

We faced a dizzying amount of changes in the first three months after the acquisition, being shuttled from one part of the company to the next. One-third of our twenty-five-person team quit within a year of the acquisition. I stayed for two years to offer some sense of continuity, while my co-founders, Darrin Massena and Mike Harrington (who were equally involved with the sale of the company to Google), continued to work at the acquired company for more than a year. By 2012, Google shut down Picnik entirely. I felt like I let a bunch of great people down.[26]

Now when entrepreneurs ask Sposato about the pros and cons of selling their companies, he advises that you look beyond the bottom line of any deal, and carefully consider how a sale will affect your team's culture. "Looking back, I should have insisted that Google's crystal ball for Picnik was clearer," he writes. "I sometimes wonder whether we should have sold the company at all."[27]

Stewart Butterfield expressed similar regrets about selling one of his early companies, photo-sharing service Flickr, to Yahoo for $25 million. Butterfield, some friends, and his then wife, serial entrepreneur and investor Caterina Fake, started Flickr as a spin-off of an online video game. Soon the product was growing so quickly that Flickr couldn't afford all the new servers it needed to host the huge amounts of photos its customers were uploading, *Inc.*'s Jeff Bercovici reports:

When Yahoo offered $25 million for Flickr, it seemed like the perfect answer. Shortly after the sale, however, Flickr got re-shuffled into a division it didn't belong in. While it languished, Facebook and YouTube rapidly overtook it as the biggest social sites. "We felt like we'd been sold a bill of goods," says [co-founder Cal] Henderson.

Butterfield gritted his teeth through three years at Yahoo, and then left in 2008, ready for a do-over. He summoned his coconspirators (minus Fake [they divorced in 2008]) and set about building a massive multiplayer game called *Glitch*. Another social fantasy game, with a narrative involving giants and time travel, *Glitch* raised $17 million from Accel Partners and Andreessen Horowitz, but the timing was again bad: They were building a desktop game at a time when users were migrating over to mobile devices. After some hard conversations, Butterfield and his partners made the decision to shut down *Glitch* in October 2012. Butterfield broke down in tears telling his staff. They offered the VCs their remaining money back, about $5 million, but were told to keep it and try to build something else with a skeleton crew.[28]

They ended up building a workplace communication tool you may have heard of: Slack. Within two years, the company had more than 1.7 million users and $45 million in annual revenue, leading *Inc.* to name Slack its 2015 Company of the Year. Less than three years later, Butterfield's latest startup had raised almost $1.3 billion and was valued by its investors at a whopping $7.1 billion.[29]

No matter how much money you're getting from a sale, be prepared for an emotional letdown once you've let go of your company. Toni Ko started Los Angeles cosmetics company NYX in 1999, when she was twenty-six, and proceeded to pour fifteen years of her life into it. In July 2014, Ko sold NYX to L'Oreal for an estimated $400 million.

"I thought: 'I'm going to sell the company and have work-life balance!' And I would travel," Ko told *Inc.*'s Christine Lagorio-Chafkin. "I thought, 'I'm going to be able to let go. I'm going to retire. I'm going to get a margarita, sit on the beach, and read a book.'"

That isn't what happened next, Ko recalled:

Selling the company took three years of preparation. It's kind of a plateau—and then there is a drop-off point. The drop-off point is the day after you sell the company.

Words cannot describe that moment. I felt like a balloon that had been filled with oxygen to its fullest, and someone came and gave it a small stab with a needle, and it just went pop. And there was nothing. Blank. Black. Dark. Hole.

I initially thought I would go and drink champagne and celebrate. But what I did the day I got the wire transfer in, and the transaction confirmed and completed, was pack my stuff from my office and walk quietly out. I went and fell asleep for, I think, fourteen hours straight.[30]

Ko recovered—by starting a new company, sunglasses seller Perverse.

If this doesn't sound dramatic enough for you, or if you want to aim for a big, ambitious, highly regulated exit—one that may still leave you as CEO—let's look at what it means to try to take your company public.

IPOS: SELLING TO
WALL STREET INVESTORS

❝ I thought about going public from day one. And I loved the whole process. I think it's made us a better company. Once you're public, good enough is not good enough. If you're good, you're expected to be great the next quarter. If you're great, then you have to be even greater. I find it inherently motivating."[31]

KEN MOELIS, cofounder and CEO of investment bank Moelis & Co., which raised $163 million in a 2014 IPO

Going public has a lot of associated hype: Taking over the New York Stock Exchange! Ringing the opening bell! CNBC hits! IPO day swag!—and much, much more red tape. By selling shares in your company to public investors, you're committing to regularly disclosing your finances, and abiding by SEC regulations, and hosting quarterly conference calls with Wall Street analysts, and all the related fun stuff.

"'Here's the issue about being a public company,' HomeAway cofounder and then-CEO Brian Sharples told *Inc.*'s Tom Foster. 'If you're private, you just make a decision. You don't have to tell anybody.' But when you're public, you do have to tell people, and include some details: 'If you're going to telegraph decisions,' he says, 'analysts need numbers to plug into their models.'"[32]

Those sorts of additional obligations aren't even the biggest reason the IPO market has been a little slow and weird the last few years. The amount of VC available to some founders has created incentives for companies to stay private as long as they can keep raising subsequent rounds, seemingly indefinitely.

As Jacqueline Kelley, EY's Americas IPO Markets Leader, writes for Inc.com:

It used to be that IPOs were an essential way to raise capital—and they're still great for that. But today there's lots of financing available, especially so-called late-stage capital, which comes even after a company has grown dramatically and has a large valuation. There's money to be had from familiar sources like venture capital and private-equity firms—and there's more of it. In 2006, $31.2 billion of venture capital money funded 2,888 private US companies, according to EY. In 2015, $77.3 billion went into 4,244 companies. But there are also a slew of new sources available for financing—including sovereign wealth funds, corporate venture funds, and a range of financial institutions around the globe that can allow a company to be awash in investments before it goes public.

That didn't used to be the case. The runway to an IPO was shorter and companies went public with lower valuations and smaller sticker prices. Today, it's common for companies to have much larger valuations before their shares are put on public exchanges. There's no reason to rush to public-equity markets just to get financing when there's a whole ecosystem of ways to get capital.[33]

Still, the US IPO market seems to be back on an upswing: Only 105 companies priced public offerings in 2016, and only 160 did last year, according to Renaissance Capital.[34] But by halfway through 2018, the pace of IPO pricings had increased and 105 companies had priced their IPOs—the same number as the total number of companies that went public in 2016.

In 2007, Lynn Jurich cofounded solar-energy company Sunrun, which installs residential solar panels and provides free maintenance on them. Homeowners then buy their power from Sunrun, which reduces their electric bill by roughly 20 percent. Jurich, the CEO, acquired 100,000 Sunrun customers in the first seven years of her company's life, and took it public in 2014 with a $251 million IPO.

"Being public has been a positive experience, because the quarterly march helps us stay focused and hit the numbers," she told *Inc.*'s Leigh Buchanan.[35] "It also gives us more visibility to talk about the financial benefits. Lack of awareness is holding this industry back."

WHAT DOES THE IPO PROCESS ENTAIL?

Hiring investment banks. Hiring lawyers. Going on a road show to pitch investors. Preparing SEC filings (and getting ready to do so forever). Preparing for a wave of press attention, as well as SEC requirements for media quiet periods. Getting ready to live and die by your company's share price. Even going through the opening-bell theater, as Zendesk cofounder and CEO Mikkel Svane recalled to *Inc.*'s Will Yakowicz:

> The day of, you're nervous. But once you're up there, you realize it's a big show. The market starts without you; the bell is fake. But the deal is the natural evolution of the company and is very real. All your employees and investors have been putting in work, and it's about building value, not to cash out but to create a connection between their work and the company's

value. We have 1,600 employees. The changes we've gone through are less about being a public or a private company and more about size. Once you grow to a couple hundred employees, you realize things need to change.[36]

As Svane, and Jurich, and investment banker Ken Moelis, and many other founders have told us, graduating to the public markets imposes an extra layer (or several) of scrutiny and accountability on your company.

Moelis, who worked in investment banking for decades before starting his own boutique firm, set up shop right as the financial crisis gathered steam. As he told me in 2018:

It was terrifying for everybody, but if you were starting a business, it was probably worse. The Monday that Lehman Brothers went down, we were meeting with a large institution that was going to make a big investment with us. I just looked at the woman from the institution and said, "Look, you're not going to do this right now. Why don't we just give it up?" She goes, "Yeah. You're right. We're not doing this." So we left the room. But we stayed friendly.[37]

Moelis & Co. weathered the banking crisis, and Ken Moelis prepared it for an IPO by 2014. "Once you're public, good enough is not good enough," is how he describes life since. "I find it inherently motivating."[38]

Other founders consider life in public to be a fun challenge: "You're insanely focused on hitting the numbers you're guiding everybody to. It gives everyone a clear goal to shoot for," says FitBit cofounder Eric Friedman.[39]

Others admit this sort of relentless focus on quarterly performance, and all the attendant scrutiny, can be a bit of a drag. "If I had another life, I'd keep my company private," Alibaba cofounder Jack Ma, who raised $25 billion in his company's 2014 IPO, said a year later.[40]

Which is one reason EY's Kelley advises not even bothering, if you're not looking at life after the opening bell.

"For any company still planning an eventual IPO, it's crucial to prepare your business to be sustainable—beyond any first-day pop in stock price," she writes in *Inc.* "Beyond financial metrics, there are more intangible indicators of IPO success. These so-called soft metrics look at the company's leadership team, which includes its founders, C-suite executives, board, and advisors. Just as sustainable companies must invest in their infrastructure, so must they invest in the right managers."[41]

If you're up to doing all of this, you might find yourself echoing the attitude of Grubhub cofounder and CEO Matt Maloney, who shrugs off concerns that going public is too much of a pain.

"I think that's bogus," Maloney told *Inc.*'s Leigh Buchanan, adding that being public has made buying other companies much easier for him. "We have over $300 million in the bank. We are really active in recruitment. Restaurants have more confidence because we're listed on the NYSE," Maloney added. "And the tactical restrictions of being public are really not that big a deal."[42]

Going public is also one way to help finance your company's growth. Though if an IPO is your goal, you'll have to think through your expansion strategy long before you ring any Wall Street bells. For a guide to the money questions you'll face while expanding your business, turn to the next chapter.

THE ECONOMICS OF EXPANDING

❝ It is very clarifying and liberating—and in hindsight, kind of fun—when the challenges facing you are making payroll and keeping the lights on. . . . You don't feel like it's a luxury when you are in it. But it feels like a luxury afterward."[1]

PHIL LIBIN, cofounder of Evernote

❝ The goal is not to envision where you'll be five or ten years from now. The goal is to envision what you'd like to get done tomorrow. And after a while you have 300 tomorrows, 600 tomorrows, 10,000 tomorrows. And all of a sudden, you are master of your domain."[2]

JESSICA O. MATTHEWS, founder and CEO of Uncharted Power

CONGRATULATIONS, YOU HAVE MONEY! You've lined up investors with deep pockets, or your business is growing so well that customer orders and payments are rolling in. You might even be—gasp!—profitable.

First, take a moment to breathe, and acknowledge your hard work. Seeing your company grow up is a triumph. You're in the black, you're making regular sales, you're not worried every day about finding customers or paying employees. And you can start to think about expanding.

All of which brings more challenges. Everything from opening new office space to bringing on additional workers can create financial and cultural growing pains, as many a founder has told us. Sometimes these are even worse than the startup pains. So, what's the right time to expand your business, and how do the most successful founders avoid financial growing pains?

What *Inc.*'s Leigh Buchanan calls your company's "awkward adolescence" involves making many more complex decisions, with fewer visible indicators that you've chosen well.

Evernote cofounder Phil Libin, for example, survived many a sleepless night during his productivity-app company's early days. In 2008, in the middle of the financial crisis, he almost ran out of

cash when an investor pulled out of a planned deal. A Swedish su-
perfan swept in and gave Evernote $500,000 to stay afloat. Three
years later, *Inc.* named Evernote its 2011 Company of the Year.[3]

But Libin, who stepped down as Evernote CEO in 2015, told
Buchanan that year that he kind of missed the stressful early days:

> Things are less focused in adolescence, since death no longer
> loiters in the lobby. Instead, decisions grow more complex,
> because options multiply, and it's harder to tell when you've
> succeeded. At that stage, "many goals are no longer externally
> imposed," says Libin. "So not only do you have the stress of
> executing, but you have the additional stress of not being sure
> the goals you have set are the correct goals."
>
> And absent life-or-death issues, "you start feeling less he-
> roic," says Libin. "The level of drama changes. It becomes
> more nuanced."
>
> But adolescence is also when companies can start making
> a real difference. "When you are a startup, your job is to be
> flashy and impressive," says Libin. As companies mature, he
> says, so should their priorities: from "optimizing for what will
> get noticed" to "optimizing for what will have the most mean-
> ingful impact."
>
> At Evernote, that meant jettisoning beloved projects, in-
> cluding a study aid and a parenting app. The key question
> for founders in this phase, says Libin, is "Are we being suf-
> ficiently epic?"[4]

If "adolescence is also when companies can start making a real
difference," how can you make sure you're ready to enter this new
phase, along with the corresponding new set of challenges?

The questions you'll face and the money you'll have to spend along the way will vary widely depending on your company, industry, and market. New challenges may involve your production processes, your physical space, the fun stuff of taxes and insurance and regulation and other red tape—and above all, your employees.

In this chapter, we'll explore the major areas you'll have to consider as your business expands—and the money you'll have to spend along the way.

JUMP-START YOUR EXPANSION

If you've already raised money, you and your investors may decide it's time for another round. If you haven't, now may be the time. If it's your first time seeking venture capital, turn back to Chapter 4.

If you're considering a subsequent round with existing or new venture investors, there's good news and bad news. The bad news first: The funding funnel narrows with every round of money startups seek.

About 70 percent of tech startups that raised venture capital failed or became self-sustaining, according to analysis by research firm CB Insights. Less than half (46 percent) of the startups tracked were able to raise a second round of funding, or series A, after the first or "seed" round.[5]

However, for startups that raise a series A, fundraising starts to get easier, according to CB Insights: 61 percent of the tracked startups that raised two rounds of financing were then able to raise a third.[6]

"I think it's so important to realize: Hey, it gets harder, not easier necessarily, to raise money. Even if you are doing well," says Frida Polli, cofounder and CEO of hiring startup Pymetrics.[7]

Polli spent a decade as a cognitive neuroscientist at Harvard and MIT before launching her company with neuroscience researcher Julie Yoo in New York in 2013. During that time, Pymetrics raised $17 million in funding from VC firms including KhoslaVentures and Jazz Venture Partners.[8]

When we spoke in July 2018, Polli was frank about the mounting difficulty of the fundraising treadmill: "Every single time you fundraise, you're basically deciding how much of the company you're giving away, to whom you're giving it away, what are the rights, what are the terms. What type of fund is really going to care about the metrics of the business versus what type of fund is going to care about, 'What's your big-picture vision—and that's all we invest in'? We're so busy operating, running the business....At the end of the day, [fundraising is] what determines the health of your business, if you don't fundraise in a way that's smart."[9]

Sometimes it can get easier. Two years after scrambling to line up its $3 million series A, the founders of robo-advisory startup Betterment found themselves fielding unsolicited offers of a series B round, according to *Inc.*'s Robin D. Schatz:

In January 2012, a representative from Menlo Ventures, a Silicon Valley VC fund, came by for a visit. Six months later Menlo's managing director, John Jarve, got in touch. Betterment wasn't looking for a second round, but [CEO Jon] Stein and his team speak to Jarve on the phone. After another call, they were invited to visit in Menlo Park. A week or so after that, Jarve flew out to New York. In October 2012, Menlo announced it would lead a group of investors, including

Bessemer and other first-round investors, in a $10 million round of Series B financing in Betterment. "We didn't think it would happen so soon," says Stein. "But we learned to be ready when you find the right investor."[10]

And the money kept on rolling in for Betterment, which by 2016 was on to its series E.[11]

The Scramble of Salad Days

Jonathan Neman stumbled into his future when he moved into his freshman-year college dorm. Nicolas Jammet, the child of high-end restaurateurs, moved in next door at Georgetown's Harbin Hall. By the end of their college years, Jammet would become Neman's cofounder. A few days later, on the first day of class, Neman met Nathaniel Ru, who would become the third cofounder of the healthy salad empire now known as Sweetgreen.

By the end of their senior year, the three friends were opening the first Sweetgreen in a tiny Georgetown space. The company's early days were a lesson in managing expectations, Neman told me on an episode of *Inc. Uncensored* podcast:

"When we first opened, we actually thought it was going to be straight to major cities. We went to LA, started looking at real estate; went to New York, started looking at real estate; we thought, within a few years, we'd have one or two locations in every major city," he recalled. "The smartest thing we ever did was to not do that. . . . For us, the restraint and the focus was something we talked a lot about. We opened the first almost-twenty restaurants in the DC area."[12]

Today, Sweetgreen has $135 million in high-profile venture backing, but Neman says the first several years of fundraising were a struggle, every time. At the beginning, the three cofounders opened the first store with $300,000.

"I call it a Kickstarter before there was Kickstarter. There were forty-five investors and $300,000," Neman says:

Most checks were around $5,000. Our biggest check was $20,000. We were talking to hundreds of people. It was the gauntlet of starting something. You had to believe in it so much that you were willing to take other people's money to do it. . . . And for us, raising money from other people from the beginning created this accountability, and wanting to do things the right way. . . .

[Raising money] the second time around, it got a lot harder, because then it was 2008 and 2009, and the world fell apart. And so then it got really, really difficult. At the time we were fundraising one restaurant; we were opening our second and third restaurant, both in DC, and it was really challenging to raise that money. It ended up being a combination of small-business loans, credit cards, some investors, we owed our contractor money so he became an investor for the money we owed him—it was very, very complicated. And it was kind of like that for the first twenty restaurants.

We kind of funded it slow and steady, really until we had that proof of concept and opened in Boston and New York, where we felt we had a brand built bigger than the business, and had a vision built for where we could go from there. And at that point is where we felt comfortable raising more money, and significant capital. That was the first time we took any sort of venture capital money. At that point it was $22 million.[13]

As Neman and his cofounders experienced, just because you've raised money from one set of people doesn't mean you're locked into returning to them for every additional thing you need. You may want to search for bank loans or other debt financing for your expansion, depending on how strong and predictable your business's cash flow is.

In 2013, Elliot Bohm, CEO of gift-card sales site CardCash.com, oversaw a $6 million series A raise from venture capital firm Guggenheim Capital. A year later, he decided to take $6 million in debt financing from a bank called Sterling National.

On Inc.com, Bohm explained that the venture capital round gave his company credibility, notably with big partners: "Once Guggenheim came on board we closed deals with Walmart, CVS, United Airlines, and InComm, all within a year." When CardCash needed more money to meet the increased demand from those partners, Bohm writes, raising more equity didn't make sense:

Here's when debt-funding works:

—Your cash flow is strong and predictable.

—You have the credibility needed to grow your business.

—You have no interest in giving away more equity. . . .

We had very predictable cash flow and could confidently pay back a loan without anxiety. We just needed to shore up for a short-term increase in demand.

Credibility certainly wasn't an issue anymore, since we had just closed a string of unbelievably beneficial partnerships.

And giving up equity was pretty low on our list of priorities. Remember, holding on to equity isn't just about maximizing your payout down the line. It's about maintaining control over strategy and operations. Equity is precious. Giving it up to capitalize on a short-term opportunity, one that could be funded just as easily with debt, is a shoddy way to run a business.[14]

Don't think that because you raised money one way in your company's early days, you're locked into that sort of financing for the life of your business. Each time you think you need the funds to expand, weigh all of your options—not just the obvious or sexy-sounding ones.

Now may also be a time to consider, or reconsider, *private-equity investment*, depending on how quickly you want to expand. Remember that PE investors tend to take majority stakes and often want control—meaning they may seek to replace you.

Though that's not always true. For instance, BlackLine founder and CEO Therese Tucker sought a private-equity investor when she was feeling burned out and ready for retirement. When she found the right buyer, Tucker felt excited to stick around—and her investors, Silver Lake Sumeru, told me they wanted her expertise as well as her company:

> "A lot of product founders don't make the transition to being the CEO of a bigger company, but Therese has a knack for figuring out when she needs to drill down and when she needs to run with things," says Hollie Moore Haynes, who led Silver Lake Sumeru's initial 2013 private equity investment in BlackLine and remains on its board. "She kept hitting numbers—and she's the heart of the company."
>
> "It didn't matter to me that she hadn't done this before," says Haynes, who's since started her own private equity firm, Luminate Capital. "We just want companies that have really great products."[15]

Sometimes taking PE money will also help you achieve a new goal, as TOMS founder Blake Mycoskie discovered. When he sold half of his pioneering "one for one" shoe company to Bain Capital in 2014, Bain helped Mycoskie establish the TOMS Social Entrepreneurship Fund to invest in social ventures. As *Inc.*'s Leigh Buchanan reports:

Mycoskie is putting more than $150 million of his own money into innovative social ventures. TOMS Social Entrepreneurship Fund has so far invested from $25,000 to $250,000 in a dozen companies whose missions range from helping homeless and disabled artists to making organic food affordable. And TOMS is experimenting with its own giving model: expanding the definition of one-for-one, venturing into local manufacturing, and tweaking its use of donations to achieve more targeted goals. With a mountain of village dust and a sprinkling of stardust, TOMS is embarking on its second act.[16]

Both Mycoskie and Bain initially contributed 1 percent of TOMS's value to endow the fund with $12.5 million, according to Buchanan. Then Mycoskie decided to really go for it: "After the deal was done, I said that's great," says Mycoskie. "But my wife and I just personally believe that half of our money"—that's $150 million—"we should invest in social entrepreneurs."[17]

Which brings us to another money question around expansion: Do you want your business to do something charitable along with its profit-seeking motives? We'll come back to this topic later in the chapter. First, let's examine how much money you are, or should be, spending.

FEEL THE BURN

"When inDinero ran out of funding and I had to lay off our staff several years ago, I learned to never read or believe your own headlines, good or bad. I got drunk off our press, and we grew and spent accordingly. Big mistake!"[18]

—

JESSICA MAH, cofounder and CEO of accounting-software company inDinero

The first rule of expanding: Don't spend money before you have to, especially not on stupid shit.

As *Inc.*'s Helaine Olen writes, startup burn rates can quickly get out of hand—particularly if you're overspending on fancy office space, or Silicon Valley–type free massages and catered meals: "Businesses should burn cash only for specific reasons, like growing to a critical mass of users or getting a product to a certain stage of development," Marc Prosser, cofounder of Marc Waring Ventures, told Olen.[19]

That's advice repeated by many a Silicon Valley veteran. "Don't spend your money just because you have it," Ellen Pao, former venture capitalist and onetime Reddit CEO, who's now cofounder and CEO of Project Include, told *Inc.*'s Kimberly Weisul. "Be frugal, because your runway is really important."[20]

That's a lesson inDinero founder Jessica Mah learned the hard way. A high school dropout who launched her financial startup at age nineteen, Mah was hailed early as a star; she graduated from Y Combinator's summer 2010 class with $1.2 million in funding and glowing headlines comparing her to Mark Zuckerberg.

The business model proved unsustainable, and Mah had hired too many close friends. Before long, she was fighting with her cofounders and running out of money. "The startup was burning through $80,000 a month, with only $150,000 left in the bank, and Mah had to lay off all her friends," *Inc.*'s Kate Rockwood reports. "We were racing our Ferrari into a brick wall," Mah admits.[21]

Fortunately, a business pivot and some marriage counseling with her (platonic) cofounder helped Mah swerve. With $2.9 million in 2014, inDinero ranked number 146 on the 2015 Inc. 500 list of the fastest-growing private companies in America.

Yet for growing companies, not spending any money isn't the answer. In its early days, one company's fundraising "was $2.5 million and lasted us two and a half years. Yes, our burn rate was that low," Pymetrics cofounder and CEO Frida Polli recalled to me recently, a bit wistfully. "If only that was still the case."[22]

At this stage of your company's life, you can't be so frugal that you undermine your own growth. Like Goldilocks, you'll have to calculate the amount of spending that's not too little or not too much, but is just right. As *Inc.*'s Jill Hamburg-Coplan reports:

> Gary Kunkle, *Inc.*'s resident economist and a specialist in long-term growth strategies, says one of the biggest reasons growth companies stumble is that they fail to invest in capacity and can't keep up with demand. Which is sobering enough—until he adds that another major pitfall for growth companies is investing too much capital to meet demand that never materializes. In that case, your capital outlay could create a burden (in leasing fees, debt payments, or depletion of precious cash) great enough to sink the business.
>
> Many entrepreneurs make the mistake of getting stuck on the niceties, wondering if the capital investment will streamline things or add convenience, says John Terry, founder of

Dallas advisory firm ChurchillTerry. Instead, Terry says, you should focus on one simple question: Will it bring money in the door? If it won't, he adds, "just put your head down and keep pushing forward."[23]

Managing cash flow gets vastly more complicated, too, even if you're profitable, thanks to your operation's additional complexity. "When you have a handful of customers, tracking down payments is easy. As your client base grows, staying on top of accounts receivable becomes more time consuming," Hamburg-Coplan writes. "New customers may insist on paying in, say, sixty days, even though rent, payroll, and other bills are due in thirty. Meanwhile, more cash is flying out the door to cover inventory, higher taxes, government-compliance expenses, and debt."[24]

If you aren't already using QuickBooks, Pulse, Float, or some other kind of cash-flow-management software, now is a good time to start.[25] Depending on how large your company is, and how complex its finances are, you may also want to consider hiring a full-time chief financial officer or head of accounting, or delegating those responsibilities.

Just don't delegate too much—even if the day-to-day numbers become someone else's responsibility, you shouldn't lose sight of them.

CREDIT CARD FEES AND
OTHER CYBER HEADACHES

Another complication of doing more in sales: paying more in credit card processing fees. If you run any sort of retail operation, online or in the real world, you know that you'll have to pay the banks a cut every time your customers buy something using a credit or debit card (or with Apple Pay, or Samsung Pay, or— you get the idea).

When we examined the finances of radically transparent tech startup Buffer, credit card processing fees were the fourth-largest monthly expense—after employee salaries, software and server costs, and taxes, but before equipment, coworking space fees, legal costs, and insurance.

Take note: Because Buffer was sending its credit card processer, Stripe, so much business, it negotiated several reductions in the processing percentage fee. "About 4 percent of Buffer's revenue now goes to Stripe, down from more than 5 percent before," *Inc.*'s Victoria Finkle reports.[26]

Credit cards also have another, less obvious, cost: chargebacks, or what happens when a customer pays for something on his or her card and then disputes the charge with the bank, rather than contacting you for a refund. Some chargebacks result from customer mistakes, bad business practices, or sloppy customer service, but an increasing amount (40 to 50 percent, according to the Kansas City Fed) result from deliberate fraud. Cybercrime is contributing to their rise, and a concurrent rise in associated costs, as *Inc.*'s Alina Tugend reports:

> The expense goes beyond just the losses themselves; associated costs, including bank fees and replacing merchandise,

are also mounting. Chargeback expenses increased 8 percent last year for all US merchants, and "for every dollar of losses, merchants are losing $2.40," a recent LexisNexis report found.[27]

You can decrease your chargeback expenses by tracking any large or unusual orders and their point or origin—especially if the IP addresses are from countries known for suspicious cyberactivity. You can also ask for verification of any suspicious transaction, or—if this becomes a big problem for your business—hire a third-party fraud-prevention firm.

Speaking of fraud-prevention vendors, you may also need to set aside some money to bulk up your cybersecurity. In 2015, 43 percent of cyberattacks were waged against small businesses, according to Symantec, and the average cost of a small-business attack is $7,000.[28]

You can improve your security by implementing safeguards such as the following:

→ Providing formal employee cybersecurity training, as most breaches still occur due to human error.

→ Setting up two-factor authentication or turning off online banking capabilities for your business bank accounts.

→ Scheduling weekly times to update your software, or delegating that responsibility to an employee or new hire.

→ Backing up your files both in the cloud and on physical drives.

You can also hire hackers to try to breach your company's systems, to see where the vulnerabilities lie—and what you can do to fix them.

Now that we've spent several paragraphs addressing credit card–related headaches, we must acknowledge that an increasing number of business owners swear by credit and debit cards—and, in some cases, only accept cards, not cash. Purchases on credit or debit cards tend to be larger than cash purchases, and processing sales only with plastic or phone apps has other advantages. (Even so, the practice can result in charges of elitism and inaccessibility to lower-income consumers, since wealthier people are more likely to have cards, and lower-income people tend to use cash.)[29]

Sweetgreen chose to go cashless in 2017. CEO Jonathan Neman explained his company's decision to go cashless on an episode of *Inc. Uncensored* podcast:

> When we first started Sweetgreen, cash was about 50 percent of our business. By the end of 2015, cash was in the single digits.
>
> No matter how much cash you have, you're running armored cars around daily. It's dirty, and our team members are spending about an hour of their time counting the cash. And for me, the part that made it a no-brainer was the safety of our team members: On average, we'd have about two armed robberies a year in our restaurants. I don't know how much people talk about that, but that happens a lot in retail, and it creates a lot of fear within the restaurants.[30]

As long as we're talking about the painful, potentially expensive headaches of expanding your business, let's discuss some things everyone loves talking about.

TAXES, INSURANCE, LAWYERS, AND OTHER FUN STUFF

" If your taxes are a surprise, you're doing it wrong."[31]

SARAH CARSON, founder and CEO of Leota

This feels like a good time to remind you that running a fast-growing company requires you to retain professional legal, tax, and financial advisors. If you haven't already, please hire some! This book is an introduction, but a general one. Depending on what your business does and where it operates, you'll have plenty of specific tax, legal, and regulatory questions that you'll need expert advice to navigate.

The recent changes to tax laws, while hailed by many small-business owners, are the most sweeping in decades. Position yourself to take advantage of them by finding an accountant who's right for your business, including its size and its industry. Otherwise you may experience something similar to what one small-business owner recently described to *Inc.*'s Helaine Olen:

> Troy Hazard, a serial entrepreneur and consultant based in Fort Lauderdale, Florida, figured he needed a new accountant when he realized the advice was flowing the wrong way. "Come tax time, I'd say, 'We haven't talked about this sort of planning or that way to structure a family trust,'" says Hazard, who's started and invested in businesses in real estate, marketing, and technology. "I'd hear, 'That's a good idea, Troy.' And then I'd think, 'I'm not supposed to have the good ideas.'"[32]

Olen recommends the following steps to find an accountant that best meets your company's needs:

→ Ask what size firm your accountant typically works with. "It's critical to know if your accountant has the experience to grow with the business—or if you're too small a potato to get attention," says Jennifer Myers, a financial advisor and the president of SageVest Wealth Management in McLean, Virginia.

→ Inquire with other business owners to recommend an accountant, and check his or her references. Also, "if you are using a certified public accountant—the highest designation—check on him or her with the national and local chapters of the American Institute of Certified Public Accountants, and look for any disciplinary actions taken by your state's board of accountancy."

→ Look for an accountant who responds promptly to any of your concerns, and who's proactive in communicating with you about any regulation changes (or, say, tax laws!) and their impact on your business.[33]

In terms of **business insurance**, yes, you'll have to spend some money. From 2014 to 2017, the average cost of a small-business insurance policy climbed more than 75 percent, to $1,281, according to Insureon.[34]

Experts advise at least taking out a **general liability policy**, which "can protect you from costs associated with a wide swath of ills, from customers' bodily injuries to libel," *Inc.*'s Kate Rockwood reports: "The average general liability policy is one of the least expensive types of coverage, according to Chicago policy provider Insureon. For a low-risk business, on average, coverage with a $1 million ceiling will set you back $425 annually."[35]

As with your search for the right accountant, ask other business owners in your industry for insurance agent recommendations, and check in with your agent regularly, to recalibrate the policies you have and need.

Also, ask your agent about specialty insurance you might need in addition to liability policies and business owners insurance. For example, if you have a lot of employees driving their own cars on company business, you should look into nonowned auto liability coverage.

As for lawyers, it's tempting to rely on the free online advice offered by Google and LegalZoom. Which doesn't always work out well, as *Inc.*'s Deirdre van Dyk points out:

> In the internet age, with Google doing your legal research and LegalZoom your contracts, you may have the illusion that your legal ducks are all in a row. This illusion seduces even those entrepreneurs trying to avoid disputes. "I always operate by what my grandmother said: 'An ounce of prevention is worth a pound of cure,'" says Matthew W. Richter, who co-owns Agora Auctions, an online coin-auction site. As a CPA, he carefully vets contracts, patrols his inbox, and deals with any potential conflicts immediately. Even so, he has faced problems. "My partner wanted to save money and used an online legal service," says Richter. "They completed the form saying we had employees in New Jersey. Which we didn't have." It took Richter a year of steady phone calls to the state to undo the glitch.[36]

Van Dyk recommends consulting a lawyer especially in these three instances:

→ When writing owner and shareholder agreements.

→ When paying someone as a contract worker rather than a full-time employee.

→ When writing or signing contracts with partners, vendors, or others.

And here's a current news item related to why you should retain a lawyer: when you're trying to hire international employees or workers who need help with visas—or if you already employ immigrant workers who may need legal help.[37]

Inc.'s Annalyn Kurtz reports that, as immigration laws and executive orders fly fast and furious, one way employers can help any affected workers is by providing them with referrals to qualified lawyers, setting up a legal-advice hotline, or, if you can afford it, covering legal fees. And set up these services so workers can access them confidentially.[38]

You'll undoubtedly encounter several other potential pain points as your company expands, some of which are presented in the next section.

THE BORING BASICS: INVENTORY, SUPPLY CHAIN, AND MANUFACTURING MANAGEMENT

> I was scared and embarrassed—I was on the brink of growing the business to failure. I had perfectly made dresses hanging on the racks there, ready to go—and I didn't have the cash to pay the vendors who had made them."[39]

SARAH CARSON, founder and CEO of Leota

Carson, as we discussed in Chapter 2, is far from the only founder to mismanage her inventory. After selling her cosmetics company, NYX, Toni Ko founded sunglasses company Perverse. It was going great at first, until one day in 2016, as *Inc.*'s Anna Hensel reports, when Ko realized she had way too much inventory—half a million pairs of sunglasses too many:

> "I completely forgot my own advice," admits Ko. "With my first business, the inventory was a slow buildup over the years, so I never felt cash-strapped. But as I started my second business, I overpurchased."
>
> Ultimately, she had to trash more than 250,000 pairs of glasses. She wasn't able to recoup the purchase price—but at least she saved tens of thousands of dollars in monthly storage fees. Ko swore that next time, she would remember her own advice. "As entrepreneurs, we know a lot and learn a lot—but sometimes we forget," she says. "And this was a crucial one for me."[40]

If you're running a products-focused business, start slow, and try to avoid overpurchasing inventory before you have orders in hand. Establishing a good relationship with your suppliers can also help you respond quickly to any new customer orders, instead of trying to buy too much product up front and hoping that the orders roll in.[41]

Conversely, pay attention to the payment agreements you have with any customers—especially, we have to say, other startups. In 2015, *Inc.*'s Graham Winfrey looked at some strategies startup founders use to protect themselves from a popping bubble:

Former venture capitalist Anand Sanwal founded private company investment database CB Insights in 2010. The data-as-a-service company helps its clients understand high-growth private companies, their investors, and their acquirers.

Sanwal advises founders with a high concentration of startup clients (or those dependent on startups for revenue) to closely monitor the financial health of those clients. Once you determine that any of them are struggling, change your payment terms. In addition to checking on things like whether they are actively hiring for new positions, look at how active they are on social media, when they issued their last press release, whether they're in a sector that is out of favor with funders, and how long it's been since they raised money. If you see a break or significant alteration in their fundraising schedule, or if they go longer than twenty-four months without a fundraising round, that's a red flag.

"If you have payment terms of thirty, sixty, or ninety days, look at tightening those up," Sanwal says. "You don't want to be left holding the bag."[42]

THE MANUFACTURING MIX

You'll have to face similar balancing acts if you're in a manufacturing-dependent business, whether you're manufacturing your own goods or with a supplier. You also need to decide where to manufacture, and whether to do it on your own or with partners, as founders of both high-tech and traditional products-based companies have told us.

"There's cost, time, and quality," Jessica Banks, founder of engineering and design firm RockPaperRobot, told *Inc.*'s Victoria Finkle. "You can usually optimize two out of the three, but you can't necessarily have all three at the same time."[43]

You may want to set up your own factory—though that's extremely expensive and likely impractical until your company gets big. Think at least $300 million to $400 million in annual sales, supply-chain consultant Bruce Tompkins told Finkle.

Outsourcing may be unpleasant for control freaks, as it involves "turning over a key part of your business and product to someone else," he says. "It's almost like getting married."[44] (There's that phrase again.)

Some founders say that outsourcing is more practical and realistic, especially if it's not your company's core competency. That's what Jessica O. Matthews, founder and CEO of alternative energy company Uncharted Power, decided.

"It was cool to bring jobs to the community, but it was hard to train workers and it wasn't really sustainable in terms of macro growth," Matthews told *Inc.*'s Donna Fenn.[45]

Instead, the Nigerian American Harvard MBA grad switched to contract manufacturing of her Socckets, soccer balls that capture kinetic energy and store it in internal generators that can power lights or phones. Matthews also worked to "make her technology scalable by shrinking it 94.5 percent in less than four years with just under $800,000 in outside funding," Fenn reported in 2016, when *Inc.* named Matthews to its 30 Under 30 list. "Shrinking the technology made the ball lighter and a bit more like a traditional soccer ball. 'In the last year, we sold over 50,000 units, putting our international supply chain and the scalability of our product to the test,' she says."[46]

Another manufacturing option, outsourcing to China or other international factories, is a practical and common manufacturing practice (as you may have heard in political news of late). Ayah Bdeir, founder and CEO of electronic-toy startup littleBits, lays out some of the practical realities of international outsourcing:

> I considered hiring a team in China to run our manufacturing operation. But if you expand to China, it becomes a matter of running two companies at once, with two offices and two teams doing quality control. I found a supply-chain partner here instead, to negotiate with manufacturers and suppliers. And so we pay an extra fee, and we give up some equity, but it's well worth it. . . . Trying to compete to make little plastic pieces cheaper here than in China—that ship has sailed. And, to be honest, it's not that interesting. There's a real resurgence of personal manufacturing here, and of high-end manufacturing of complex devices. I think that's where the US can really stand out.[47]

This was in 2015, before any new tariffs or other recent trade developments, so do the math with your accountant before setting up manufacturing anywhere.

Take comfort in the knowledge that even international celebrities and Olympic champions struggle with manufacturing decisions. Venus Williams, for example, rebooted her ten-year-old fashion brand, EleVen by Venus, around 2015. The tennis superstar had long been interested in the fashion industry, signing a big endorsement deal with Reebok in the late '90s and then, after Reebok sold to Adidas, launching her EleVen line with the Steve & Barry's chain, which imploded during the recession. "Then

Williams made a deal with a company in Los Angeles to do manufacturing for EleVen while she handled design. But without adequate distribution, among other issues, it was a losing game," *Inc.*'s Jeff Haden and Bill Saporito report.[48]

In 2015, Williams rebooted the brand, buying out her manufacturing partner and assuming sole ownership. Manufacturing has continued to be a struggle, she acknowledged in 2017: "Last year we thought we didn't have all the in-house expertise we needed to support all of our production needs, so we decided to outsource some of that . . . and we should have been more hands-on and kept production in-house," she told Haden and Saporito. "Perhaps I'm not a production expert, but since then I've learned a ton."[49]

Even with those stumbles, Williams managed to triple sales at EleVen in 2016. "I love to see things grow," she says. "I love ideas. I love putting things together. I would also like to be seen as a flexible leader, someone who can adapt and change and grow and help the people around her succeed too."[50]

NEW OFFICES, NEW STORES, AND OTHER PHYSICAL SPACES

> " Rent for our first office was $6,000 per month—and we didn't have revenue yet! We had only five people at the time, but we furnished it to fit fourteen, and we sublet the extra desks for $500 per month each."[51]

STEPH KOREY, Away CEO and cofounder

Many a founder starts his or her company in a coworking space these days, whether WeWork or The Wing or The Riveter or Spacious's network of restaurants-by-night, coworking-spaces-by-day. (I've had meetings with founders who have memberships at both WeWork and The Wing; they meet women at the latter, a women-only space, and meet the guys at WeWork.)

One way to expand is by staying in-house at a coworking space. Some of these coworking companies manage floors or entire buildings. IBM and Verizon both have employees in offices designed and run by WeWork. But depending on how fast your company is growing, and how many people you're hiring, you may one day have to consider renting your own office.

Which gets expensive, particularly if you're in high-cost urban centers like San Francisco or New York. Depending on what your company does, you may try to hire only remote workers. Buffer, a social-media analytics startup, closed its San Francisco office in October 2015, since few of its then staff of sixty-four employees were coming in regularly. Instead, Buffer purchased coworking space for any employees who wanted an office instead of a kitchen table.[52]

Some experts worry that a lack of physical office space can affect culture. Marc Effron, president of Talent Strategy Group, told *Inc.*'s Victoria Finkle that having a central workspace can encourage more "face-to-face collaboration."[53]

If you run a retailer or another type of business that requires physical space to sell its goods, of course you'll also have to consider the costs of adding new (or any!) locations. Companies that started as online-only sellers—such as Away, Casper, Glossier, Rent the Runway, and Warby Parker—have started opening showrooms or full stores.

As *Inc.*'s Graham Winfrey reports about Warby Parker, the eyeglasses startup:

> Customers sent emails asking to come to the company's offices to try on glasses. Warby Parker didn't have offices—so [Neil] Blumenthal invited customers to his apartment. The demand gave the cofounders the confidence to open shops within boutique retailers and launch the Warby Parker Class Trip, a store built into a school bus that visited fifteen cities. "We were able to explore different neighborhoods in each one of those cities, so it gave us a blueprint and data for where to open up stores," Blumenthal says. In April 2013, Warby Parker opened its first, in New York City's SoHo.[54]

Still, taking the plunge into real-world stores can be expensive. "We'd never spent that kind of money!" is how Parachute founder and CEO Ariel Kaye describes the five-year lease and security deposit for her first real-world store. Kaye founded the bedding-and-bath company in 2014 as an online-only, direct-to-consumer model—even though, historically, 90 percent of sales in the bedding and bath categories have come from in-store purchases.

As *Inc.*'s Christine Lagorio-Chafkin reports, Parachute's initial lean model "had been built around the idea it needn't rent costly retail space or hire store employees. And Parachute's model already was working: With a mere $15 million in funding from investors, it had consistently launched new and successful products. It was moving toward profitability, and had sold more than $1 million in bedding online each of the past two years."[55]

Kaye agonized over the expense of moving into the real world, and the more than $100,000 she would need to spend to build out her first store. But eventually, she pulled the trigger. And then opened more stores. And then made her company profitable—thanks in no small part to in-store repeat customers.

"I felt a lot of pressure and stress to make the right decisions—and in retrospect, that wasn't helpful at all," Kaye told Lagorio-Chafkin. "That's something I really learned from."

Casper CEO Philip Krim told me that when his mattress company was selling mattresses online exclusively, people would swing by the company's New York headquarters and ask if they could test out the mattress. Soon Casper started designing pop-up stores and looking into more permanent retail locations.

Those also took some adjustment. At first, Krim and his co-founders didn't expect people to want to carry a mattress out of the store with them—and Casper hadn't planned for places that have a lot of inventory storage space:

> We thought people would just lie on the bed and then we'd deliver it. But customers would say, "I'd like to take the bed," and we'd be like, "Uh-oh, we don't have inventory." That forced us to rethink how we build stores—because now we have to keep inventory. Another thing we didn't account for: So many folks were coming that there was a wait to try mattresses in some stores.[56]

The New York–based company, which had nineteen stores by July 2018, now has displays and videos to entertain customers while they wait to try the beds.

BUYING OTHER COMPANIES

❝ I love Monopoly. You know why? When I play Monopoly with you, I'm going to buy everything from Baltic Avenue to Marvin Gardens. If you get to my side of the board, you'd better roll boxcars or you're going to pay rent."[57]

___

KEVIN PLANK, founder and CEO of Under Armour

We've discussed how to sell your company—but what if you're ready to buy someone else's?

"If we wanted to expand somewhere and we knew there was already a competitor dominating the market in that area, then we would consider what would be cheaper: trying to beat them on their territory, or make a deal and buy them," Inc.com columnist Bill Green, founder and CEO of The Crestar Group of Companies and LendingOne, writes of his time running a previous company. "Every market, every region, was a buy-or-build decision."[58]

He further explains:[59]

In some cases, you can look at acquisitions as a way of just buying your ideal customer.

Yes, you're buying a company, but once you acquire it, what you're really buying is their book of business. You might not need their CFO, because you already have one. Or, you might not need their offices because you already have offices in those areas. So it's not so much that you're buying the infrastructure, as much as you are buying their customers—which you can then roll into your already working machine.

Another example would be if you're competing for market share in a certain area, and you view the acquisition as a way to "own" that area. If there is already a competitor in the area, you could spend millions on marketing and still not dent their business. In that case, it may be better to just strike a deal and acquire your competitor. This is one of the reasons I advise so many young entrepreneurs to reinvest into their business and not take out unreasonably high salaries.

You're going to want cash on hand to strike deals like this, and expand your business.[60]

Kevin Plank, a former Division I college football player who bootstrapped his performance sportswear company in 1995, has since taken Under Armour public. In 2017, the Baltimore company employed almost 16,000 employees and garnered nearly $5 billion in annual revenue.

Plank, who remains CEO, has spent the past few years spending hundreds of millions of dollars buying "leading makers of activity- and diet-tracking mobile apps," including MyFitnessPal, *Inc.*'s Tom Foster reports. "By doing so, the company has amassed the world's largest digital health-and-fitness community, with 150 million users. Plank envisions all of those users, and their metrics, as a big data engine to drive everything from product development to merchandising to marketing."[61]

Another Monopoly player extraordinaire is Amazon founder and CEO Jeff Bezos, who's bought everything from newspapers to grocery stores in recent years. In May 2017, right before news of its Whole Foods deal broke, *Inc.*'s Zoe Henry looked at 128 start-ups that Amazon had purchased or invested in:

What's driven the Seattle behemoth to sink its tentacles into such a broad range of upstarts? "When Amazon decides it wants to win something and the market's important to it, it will try to compete. If it can't, it will ultimately buy the leader," says Jeremy Levine, a partner at venture capital firm Bessemer Venture Partners, a shareholder in Quidsi, which Amazon purchased in 2011 (and shuttered in March).

Common themes among the companies Amazon has brought into its inner circle: startups that adopted the retailer's technology early on; that help put it in direct orbit of Apple, Google, and Netflix; or that vault it into a new geography or category, as it's doing with its more recent Alexa Fund, which is funneling $100 million into artificial intelligence startups. While Amazon has had its share of winning bets like Zappos and Evi, if you ever get the chance to pitch Bezos, you might not want to remind him of LivingSocial.[62]

We don't recommend trying to match Amazon's deal-making appetite until you're close to matching its revenues. However, even at a small scale, you can follow some of its strategy in seeking acquisitions that help you expand or that make sense given a preexisting relationship with the company you're looking at buying.

Then, if you want the acquisition to succeed and to help your bottom line, a lot of the same advice applies to buyers and sellers. *Inc.*'s Adam Bluestein addresses two specific aspects to manage during the process:

→ **Hold on to key people,** through both informal methods (communicating with and listening to the acquired employees, sometimes allowing them to stay in the same physical locations) and equity incentives. "It is very common to have part of the acquisition price paid in some form of retention, where critical employees must stay to earn it," says Ted Wang, an attorney with Fenwick & West, whose clients include Facebook, Twitter, and Dropbox.

→ **Take integration slow,** especially if you want to ape the success of the corporate buyers of startups we've discussed in previous chapters. "The people who excel at building something from scratch rarely overlap with the people who want to work in the belly of a megacorporation under two new layers of management," says David Heinemeier Hansson, cofounder and CTO of software maker Basecamp.[63]

THE MARKETING QUESTION

Social media, Facebook algorithms, data privacy concerns, and the rise of the influencer age have all contributed to making marketing a fraught—and potentially expensive—area for your business. By early 2017, "according to social-media analytics firm Captiv8, companies are shelling out an estimated $225 million per month for sponsored posts on Instagram alone," *Inc.'s* Kate Rockwood reports.[64]

Despite the expense, marketing is crucial for most businesses. Fortunately, *Inc.* has already written a whole book about this topic! According to author Simona Covel, most experts recommend setting a marketing budget that's between 1 percent and 10 percent of your sales. That will vary depending on your industry, what you can afford, and how established your company is. According to Covel, some experts even recommend that very early companies spend up to 15 percent of their sales on marketing.

Covel also explains two of the numbers you should know to help you determine your marketing budget:

It helps to start with your customer acquisition cost (CAC). That's the average cost of acquiring a new customer. Determining your CAC is easy: Add up all your sales and marketing costs for a specific period and then divide by the number of new customers landed during that period.

If you spend $100 and acquire ten customers, your CAC is $10.

What's a good number? That's harder to answer. It really depends on your industry and business model. It's also important to understand how CAC fits into your overall operating budget. The leaner your operation overall, the more you can afford to spend to acquire a customer. Plus, the longer you hang on to customers in general, the more you can justify on each new customer acquisition. That's a customer's lifetime value, or LTV, which can be defined as the profit your company can expect to generate from a customer, multiplied by the typical amount of time you hang onto the customer (e.g., *x* number of years).

Once you've built a little history you can start to spot customer retention and spending trends. Then the math gets a lot easier: Determine what the average customer spends over a specific time period and calculate the return on your original customer acquisition cost investment.[65]

For even more advice on effective marketing strategies and spending, we encourage you to consult Simona Covel's *Marketing Your Startup: The* Inc. *Guide to Getting Customers, Gaining Traction, and Growing the Business.*

FIGURE OUT YOUR OWN SALARY

" When the money started coming in, Ken and I didn't pay ourselves for another year. Instead, we bought more equipment and expanded next door."[66]

JACQUES TORRES, New York City chocolatier

You should probably wait until your business is generating ongoing sales before you give yourself a paycheck. Then, keep it low: 40 percent of the CEOs responding to our 2017 survey started themselves out with salaries of less than $50,000, which tracks with what experts recommend. As *Inc.*'s Victoria Finkle reports:

> Once you're bringing in revenue, look back at what you've earned over the past three to six months and see if you consistently have enough left over to pay yourself something like $2,500 per month, advises Brad Farris, principal advisor at Anchor Advisors, a Chicago-based small-business consultancy.
>
> That works out to about $15 per hour (for a traditional forty-hour workweek, which you'll probably still exceed). Set up a formal payroll system for yourself, taking out applicable taxes to avoid trouble with the IRS, which expects business owners to pay themselves a reasonable salary that can be taxed. This sort of setup has the added benefit of instilling a sense of discipline, which you'll need once you start taking on employees.
>
> "That's a pressure you're putting on your company of 'I need to be able to pay myself this much,'" says Farris. "When

you start hiring people, they're going to want to get paid every month." You can then take out additional funds as dividends or distributions on a monthly or quarterly basis.[67]

Brianna Wu, video game designer and studio founder, Gamergate survivor and recent congressional candidate, told *Inc.*'s David Whitford in 2015 that she still didn't pay herself anything out of her business. Instead, she and her husband, Frank, live in a house that belongs to her husband's uncle, who "lets them live there rent-free because they renovated it themselves," Whitford reports. "For the sake of keeping the three full-time members of her staff employed, Brianna has never collected a paycheck, which leaves her dependent on Frank's salary as a patent specialist with a Boston biotech firm."[68]

All of which brings us to the big cost, and its related expenses, of expanding your business: employees. The next chapter can serve as a guide about the major money questions around your workers.

7

EVERYTHING EMPLOYEE

"Don't try to hire the best people at first. If you try to hire the best when you're still a small company, it's like putting a Boeing 747 engine into a poor tractor. It won't work. But you can hire the right people, the people who know better than you, who are passionate about what they do, and who are open-minded about learning. And then when your company gets bigger, you have to rotate your people through different jobs. Make sure the engineers know about more than engineering. Work with the entire staff to make sure they are the best in their field. I have a great team, because they get everything done better than I could. So I can spend a lot of time thinking about the future."[1]

JACK MA, cofounder and executive chairman of Alibaba

CREATING JOBS. PAYING SALARIES and/or hiring contractors. Retaining, promoting, and giving raises to employees. Providing health insurance, retirement plans, paid vacation and family leave, and all the perks you can afford.

All this costs a lot of money. For example, in 2016, tech startup Buffer told us that 69 percent of its monthly expenses came from paying base salaries and payroll taxes. That's not including what it spent on insurance for the business and for employee healthcare; coworking space for those who didn't wish to work remotely; computers and other equipment for employees; or perks, including annual all-staff retreats.[2]

Some of those expenses are obviously more discretionary than others. As Ellen Pao warns in a recent question-and-answer feature with *Inc.*'s Kimberly Weisul: "You don't want employees who are there just because you're spending a ton of money on events or on alcohol or on a fancy chef. You want people who are at your company to do their work, and not for the fringe benefits. Focus on giving them great work to do, and valuing the work that they are doing."[3]

Jack Ma's first startup was scrappy. The Alibaba cofounder and executive chairman grew up teaching himself English by offering foreign visitors tours of his hometown, Hangzhou, in eastern China. Then, after a 1995 visit to Seattle, Ma returned to China determined to start an internet business. Ma, his wife, and one of his colleagues at the local university established a web design company that would make international websites for Chinese companies, so international customers could find the sites. It was rough going at first, Ma told me:

> Nobody wanted to try it. But I had a friend, Maggie Zhou, who later became my secretary and now is our [Alibaba] ambassador to Australia. She worked for a hotel called the Wanghu [Lakeview], the first four-star hotel in Hangzhou. I told her manager that I could make the hotel a free homepage, "and if there are any people who come to your hotel through that homepage, you can pay me." He agreed. And nothing happened for three months.
>
> Then the Fourth World Conference on Women was held in Beijing. Suddenly the hotel got a fax from several American ladies. They were coming to the conference and using the internet to search for hotels—and the only one listed in China was the Wanghu Hotel. We had to tell them that the hotel was more than 1,000 kilometers from Beijing. But they asked, "Can we stay in that hotel and have meetings?" After the conference, they flew to Hangzhou to stay for three days. That shocked the general manager of the hotel—and then he paid us.[4]

That sort of work and patience paid off for Ma when he gathered seventeen friends and started Alibaba, an online marketplace that's now one of the world's largest internet companies.

Depending on your business type, you may be able to grow without much hiring at first. More companies are staying lean as they grow, as *Inc.*'s Leigh Buchanan writes:

> The data shows that fast-growing companies are hiring fewer people, even as revenue swells. . . . In 1997, about 3 percent of firms with 10 or more employees had notched at least 20 percent annual employment growth over three years, reports the Bureau of Labor Statistics. By 2012—the most recent year for which data is available—that share had fallen roughly one-third. That same year, the average number of employees added from a company's launch through year five hit the lowest level since the 1990s, according to the Kauffman Foundation. That level has risen since, but it's still far below where it was in the '80s. New and growing companies are the most prolific job creators, but the number of jobs they create is falling.
>
> Despite the warm feelings generated by creating jobs, employees are a cost—something businesspeople want to minimize. What's changing is companies' ability to get by with fewer and fewer people thanks to the (growing) litany of tasks that can be digitized and automated. In 2018, building for success increasingly means building lean.[5]

Lean is only practical in some industries, or for so long. You'll have to consider several major expenses as you hire people to work in your business.

SALARIES AND COMPENSATION

" From the beginning, my goal at Chobani was not to build just a product—but to build a culture. To build tomorrow's company. I had the idea back in 2008 to share the company, 10 percent of its value, with the employees. I come from a background of farming, and I've always been angry about how ordinary working people are not recognized for their contributions. But we built this together! . . . Taking all of that credit would not be fair."[6]

HAMDI ULUKAYA, founder and CEO of Chobani

The son of Turkish sheep farmers, Hamdi Ulukaya immigrated to the United States in 1994 to study business and English, and settled in upstate New York. In 2005, he saw an ad for an abandoned yogurt-making facility, and thus was born the idea for Chobani, now the top-selling brand of Greek yogurt in the United States.

In recent years, Ulukaya has made headlines for hiring refugees and, in 2016, for giving employees shares in his company. "And the company is different because of it," he told *Inc.*'s Christine Lagorio-Chafkin. "The staff was always proud, but this ownership piece was missing. This is probably one of the smartest, most tactical things you can do for a company. You're faster, you're more passionate. Your people are happier."[7]

Whether or not you follow the example of Chobani—or of supermarket chain Publix and convenience store Wawa, both of which have employee stock ownership plans (ESOPs)—employees are a crucial part of most growing businesses' success. If you want to maintain the growth, you'll need to ensure that they feel fairly compensated.

The good and bad news is that employee compensation isn't just about money. (It might be simpler if it were!) But a lot of it comes back to money, even if it's not being spent directly on employee salaries and benefits.

Inc., along with Quantum Workplace, annually surveys thousands of employees at small businesses across the country, to find America's best workplaces. Some of the companies we've recognized in the past few years include business software maker Asana,[8] with three hundred employees, perks including kombucha on tap, generous family leave, and a culture of radical transparency and shared responsibility; online lender CommonBond,[9] which devotes part of its student loan revenues to an education nonprofit and also gives employees monthly help with their own student loan payments; and sustainable-building consultancy Lord Green Real Estate Strategies, which provides a dog-friendly office, at-work composting bins, and a lot of trust in its employees to be responsible human beings. As *Inc.*'s Tom Foster reports about how founder Mychele Lord built her consultancy:

> Nobody set any rules, for instance, about who would clean up after the dogs in the yard; it just happens. When staff wanted to start composting at work so they could take buckets of organic waste home to feed their gardens, Lord responded, "Great. I'll buy the bins, and then you're responsible for it. I'm not going to clean it up and I'm not going to hire somebody."[10]

In picking the best workplaces, *Inc.* and Quantum Workplace look at factors such as employee engagement, as well as how well companies "look after their staff's financial security through retirement, insurance, and other financial benefits. We also explore work arrangements that increase employee satisfaction, such as flextime and unlimited vacation time," as Quantum CEO Greg Harris explained.[11]

Here are some questions to consider as you hire and promote employees and set their pay, if you want your company to one day qualify as a Best Workplace:

Are you hiring salaried employees or contract workers? And are you sure you're classifying your hires correctly? If you stick to classifying your employees as salaried, instead of contractors, you'll avoid the legal and headline headaches that have plagued Uber, Lyft, Handy, Instacart, and many other "gig economy" employers. Also, when deciding how to compensate your workers, it's a good idea to err on the side of decency—it will both help you attract better talent and serve as a competitive advantage.

Are you abiding by all federal, state, and city laws about minimum wages, paid sick time, paid leave, and other benefits? In the past few years, several changes have been enacted at both state and local levels, so consult a lawyer if you're unsure about what you're obligated to provide workers.

Are you being fair, transparent, and equitable about promotions, wages, and pay? Avoid the gender pay gap, help morale, and avoid more of those negative headlines by being transparent about your salaries, and by working to redress any discovered inequities. Your business will reap the benefits of retaining employees longer and seeing their productivity increase. As *Inc.*'s Helaine Olen writes:

American women earn 82 cents for every dollar earned by men, according to Pew, and women in general are doing far worse at some big multinational companies, which pay them as little as half of what they pay men, according to recent disclosures forced by new British regulations.

Other big companies, including Starbucks and Salesforce, have acknowledged gender pay gaps and have taken concrete steps to eliminate them. This has benefits beyond good PR: Companies that prioritize pay equity are seeing worker productivity increase 19 percent above industry averages, according to Aptitude Research Partners, while employees who perceive a pay gap are 16 percent more likely to leave their companies, according to a 2017 CEB/Gartner survey.[12]

Several experts recommend making salary data fully transparent to all employees, to help prevent the appearance of a gap, and to develop and share a formula for promotions and raises.[13]

Do you want to provide employees with equity in your company? It may be a good idea to follow the lead of Chobani, Publix, Wawa, and many newer companies. AngelList, a site for investors and job seekers in such companies, provided data to *Inc.*'s Jill Krasny showing that 80 percent of job postings from US startups involve some equity.[14]

"I witnessed the passion and loyalty that came with people feeling like an owner in the business," Marc Lore, cofounder of the shopping site Jet.com and the e-commerce platform Quidsi, told Krasny, before he sold Jet to Walmart:

> Lore offers equity to Jet's entire workforce, regardless of an employee's position or time spent with the company. There's a four-year vesting period, and each position gets a standardized slug of stock—and Lore sees its impact on his workers. "They're going way beyond their day job," he says. "Working nights and weekends, and not feeling like it's a burden."[15]

If you think you want to give your employees a chance to share in ownership of your company, educate your workers up front about how they can cash out their shares and what happens if they leave the company. And do get expert advice from your accountant and lawyers before trying to set up an employee equity plan.

HEALTHCARE, RETIREMENT, AND OTHER BENEFITS

Ah, healthcare—the third rail of American policy, the bane of many small-business owners' existence, and one of the fastest-moving targets for financial experts trying to predict the regulatory landscape for business owners.

As of July 2018, the Affordable Care Act still existed and required any business with fifty or more full-time-equivalent workers for one year or more to offer health insurance. And many owners of smaller businesses still choose to take on those costs even if the law doesn't require it, reasoning that providing health insurance for their workers is both the right thing to do and a competitive advantage in hiring and retaining workers.

"About half of businesses that aren't legally required to give their workers the option of signing up for coverage offer it anyway," *Inc.*'s Helaine Olen reports, quoting a business owner who had made that decision. Mickey Swortzel, cofounder of Ann Arbor, Michigan–based New Eagle Consulting, which employs twenty-five people, told Olen, "It's a necessary benefit to attract the team we want."[16]

Whatever the state of healthcare law as you're reading this, if you have a relatively small staff and are researching ways to best provide them with health insurance, we recommend looking into professional employer organizations (PEOs). PEOs specialize in providing human resources services to other businesses, taking over the paperwork and red tape of negotiating with health insurers, retirement providers, and other service providers. ADP is the largest PEO; others include TriNet, Paychex, Justworks, and Oasis Outsourcing.

The larger scale of PEOs means they can negotiate with insurance companies and other service providers to offer you more benefits and at lower prices than you might find on your own for your business. As Olen writes:

> A company agrees to allow a PEO to process its payroll, and, in turn, the PEO becomes the employer of record for those employees. With thousands—sometimes hundreds of thousands—of "employees," PEOs are able to offer their member companies everything from health insurance to retirement benefits at much better prices than are usually available to standalone smaller firms.[17]

Which brings us to another table-stakes benefit for growing businesses: a **retirement plan** for your employees.

Figuring out the best retirement plan on your own can be headache inducing, to say the least. According to *Inc.*'s Kathy Kristof: "Once a for-profit business has more than ten or fifteen workers, the best retirement-plan options are likely to boil down to two: the simple (savings investment match plan for employees) IRA and the 401(k). Both give you the ability to contribute to your own retirement and provide attractive benefits for employees. The more highly paid workers you have, the more the 401(k) makes sense—though it also requires some truly epic paperwork."[18]

Only 5 percent of very small businesses (with between one and four employees) offer a retirement plan, according to the US Government Accountability Office, but 31 percent of slightly larger companies (twenty-six to one hundred employees) do.[19] If you're growing quickly, and hiring a lot, you'll start fielding many questions from job candidates about what sorts of retirement plan you offer.

Consult an accountant and a financial planner, especially if your business doesn't yet have a human-resources department (or employee). If you're already working with a PEO for health insurance, that firm can probably advise you on retirement plans as well.

And remember that you're not just making decisions for your workers—you're also making decisions for your own financial future, at least as your business gets off the ground. (We'll discuss more sophisticated options for your **personal retirement planning** in Chapter 8.)

Small Girls PR, a New York public-relations firm that Bianca Caampued and Mallory Blair opened in 2010, spent its first five years without a retirement plan. By the time it had hired almost twenty people, Small Girls started receiving lots of requests for help with retirement savings, which was a daunting challenge for Kara Silverman, Small Girls' director of operations. "I'd never been in the position of evaluating 401(k) plans before," she told *Inc.*'s Helaine Olen.[20]

Silverman picked a plan provider called ForUsAll, which offered retirement plans that kept costs down for both Small Girls and its employees. You'll want to look for something similar: a plan that keeps your costs down by charging you a low monthly flat fee per worker covered by the plan, rather than a percentage that will balloon as employee savings increase; and that simultaneously minimizes costs for your employees by offering them low-cost index funds.

Several newer, tech-savvy firms—including Betterment for Business, Guideline, and America's Best 401k—tend to charge less than the 1.5 to 4 percent of assets that was once standard.

Depending on how large your company is, you may even want to look at the retirement-plan offerings from better-known names. The country's largest traditional 401(k) providers, including Fidelity Investments and Vanguard Funds, offer low-cost options and some products specifically tailored for small businesses. They also offer products that can make more sense at scale. Vanguard, for example, charges an up-front service fee plus a per-employee fee, a setup that can be expensive when you're starting out, but can make sense once you have more employees.[21]

Good options exist, if you take the time to look for them, as Olen reports:

> If you're a smaller employer, you're probably going to have to search harder for affordable retirement-plan options. They do exist—as do the resources to help you find them. Index funds tend to be the cheapest and best investment for many employees' long-term retirement plans—though salespeople may try to push more expensive, actively managed funds. Or they may emphasize the bells and whistles rather than the underlying product. . . .
>
> While those working for large corporations often pay annual fees of less than 0.5 percent of the funds invested in their employee retirement plans, small-business participants can lose up to 2 percent, or even more, to expenses each year, according to BrightScope.[22]

BrightScope is one of several resources you can consult for more information about the best retirement plans for your small business. The startup evaluates 401(k) plans using publicly available data, and runs a site (https://www.brightscope.com/) that provides information about best practices and how similar-size plans compare. Other resources to help with your retirement-planning decisions include the following:

- → PlanVision and other advisory services that help companies evaluate their current retirement plans, pinpoint ways to save money, and assist in looking at proposals from retirement-plan providers.

- → Employee Fiduciary, a low-cost and transparent plan provider that publishes fees for its services on its website.

- → Investing startup Personal Capital, which has an online tool that allows individuals to check their 401(k)'s fees.

- → Robo-advisory startups such as Wealthfront and Betterment, which provide automated retirement plan services.

Paid Time Off and Parental Leave

These are another set of hot topics, which vary depending on where your business and your workers are. But as our annual Best Workplaces list demonstrates, companies that offer generous leave to their workers tend to prosper more than those that try to limit employees' paid time off. As *Inc.*'s Bartie Scott reported in 2017: "A study by The Center for American Progress found that cities and states with mandatory paid leave laws haven't seen a significant increase in unemployment. Of the nineteen localities that adopted paid sick leave policies between 2007 and 2015, unemployment did not significantly increase. Nor did it rise in any of the three states that passed paid family and medical leave laws."[23]

As of May 2018, ten states and Washington, DC, require private companies to provide employees with paid sick leave.[24] The federal Family and Medical Leave Act (FMLA)[25] requires employers with at least fifty employees to provide up to twelve weeks of unpaid leave, and states including California, New Jersey, and Rhode Island have programs that provide financial support for new parents to take time off, according to *Inc.*'s Saki Knafo:

> Offering paid parental leave can pay dividends: A 2011 report by the US Census Bureau found that women who got paid leave were more likely to return to work within five months than those who didn't receive or use the benefit. . . .
>
> Molly Moon Neitzel, founder of Molly Moon's Homemade Ice Cream, a chain of ice cream shops in Seattle with $5.4 million in 2015 sales, used a generally accepted average cost for replacing an employee ($12,000) to set her parental leave terms. She offers twelve weeks of fully paid leave, which costs a little bit less than replacing one of her highest-earning workers.[26]

Workplace Perks and More Fun Stuff

Much like parental leave, it can be financially daunting to contemplate matching the headline-grabbing benefits available at Apple, Google, and other giant tech companies: Egg-freezing costs covered! Six months of paid family leave! Unlimited vacation!

Though on that last point, *Inc.*'s Minda Zetlin reports: "Nielsen research shows employees who vacation are happier with their jobs, more engaged, and less likely to quit—or have a heart attack—than their nonvacationing peers. Those who skip vacations are also likelier to be depressed, and to dent office morale."[27]

Even if you can't match the largesse of Silicon Valley giants, *Inc.*'s Diana Ransom writes:

Even on a more modest scale, providing volunteering opportunities, fitness stipends, or spa services can help attract and retain workers. "Implementing these types of programs shows employees that their company is prioritizing their well-being and investing in their careers," says Great Place to Work's Michael C. Bush.[28]

Company retreats are one place where you might want to consider splurging, judiciously. For example, Kara Goldin, founder and CEO of flavored-water company Hint, recently flew her forty-nine employees from San Francisco to Scottsdale, Arizona, "where they spent half a week hiking, whitewater rafting, and having other outdoor fun." *Inc.*'s Helaine Olen reports that the retreat had an immediate payoff: "People jumped right back into work when it was over," Goldin recalls. "And then on the weekly conference calls, people were communicating more."[29]

Finally, we shouldn't have to say this, but since it's apparently not obvious to many employers:

Don't Harass Your Employees

It's abusive, destructive to morale, and expensive: $165 million was collected by the EEOC (Equal Employment Opportunity

Commission) from offending firms in 2015 for workers alleging harassment, *Inc.*'s Minda Zetlin reports.[30] That was *before* the ongoing #MeToo movement started to empower more women to come forward with their stories of common harassment or other unwanted sexual attention (affecting at least 60 percent of women in the workforce, according to the EEOC).

To ensure your company is doing everything possible to prevent workplace harassment, you should also take the following steps:

→ **Formalize a written sexual harassment policy,** and review it at least every three to five years.

→ **Require company-wide training once a year,** and require yourself, your CEO, and all top managers to attend.

→ **Respond immediately to any complaints.**

→ **Be willing to terminate employees, even key personnel,** over credible, serious complaints about harassment and sexual abuse.

How you handle employee complaints over this major issue, as well as minor matters, will affect how engaged your employees are and, as a result, how productive they are. And as one might expect, these situations impact your company's finances, as *Inc.*'s Paul Keegan reports:

Just 30 percent of American workers are engaged at work, according to Gallup, costing the nation $450 billion to $550 billion per year in lost productivity. (That includes the price of absenteeism, workplace accidents, and increased health-care costs.) Even the best companies—those scoring in the top 10 percent on employee surveys—register only about 38 percent of their employees as "fully engaged," according to consultant Kevin Sheridan, author of *Building a Magnetic Culture*.[31]

Keegan also cites Stanford and UC Santa Barbara research indicating that MBA grads are willing to relinquish thousands of dollars in salary to work for socially responsible companies. Which brings us to the subject of philanthropy.

HOW DO YOU WANT TO GIVE BACK?

For every pair of glasses Warby Parker sells, it makes a donation to its nonprofit partners—including VisionSpring—so people in the developing world can get eye exams and glasses cheaply. Last year, Warby distributed its millionth pair of glasses through its "buy a pair, give a pair" program—another example of how far the company has come. Now [cofounder Neil] Blumenthal wonders, "How do you scale a brand with integrity?" Like a lengthy waiting list, there are worse problems to have.[32]

Do you want to formally make your company work for a greater good than profits? Whether you call this "social good" or "for-profit, for-good" or "win-win-win" (please don't) or talk about "people, planet, profits" (again, no), many a small business these days is setting itself up with an explicitly charitable side message. Many of them are following the path forged by TOMS, which famously established the "one for one" model: For every pair of shoes the company sold, it also donated a pair to in-need children in developing countries.

A serial entrepreneur who was running an online driver's ed business in 2006, TOMS founder Blake Mycoskie created a business and a movement when he vacationed in Argentina. During a volunteer visit to deliver shoes to low-income children, Mycoskie was shaken by the poverty he saw, and envisioned a business that would supply shoe donations "through commerce rather than charity," as *Inc.*'s Leigh Buchanan puts it. "His solution is elegance incarnate: Sell a shoe, give a shoe."[33]

TOMS went on to introduce that model with other products. In 2016, Buchanan looked at the legacy and challenges of the TOMS model established by Mycoskie[34]:

> At least forty one-for-one businesses have sprung up in TOMS's wake, selling (and donating) everything from medical scrubs (Figs) to pet food (Bogo). Taking critiques of straight donations to heart, some are following TOMS's lead by supplementing or replacing straightforward product gives (TOMS 1.0) with more dimensional offerings (TOMS 2.0). . . .
>
> In the ten years since he founded the Los Angeles–based TOMS—whose revenue for the twelve months ending last June 30 was estimated by Moody's to be $392 million—Mycoskie has accumulated enough karmic capital to disappear for a week or two in pursuit of spiritual healing. His for-profit company has brightened more than fifty-one million lives with new shoes, restored vision, clean water, and safe births. Whoever writes the four-decade history of for-profit social ventures will devote a chapter to TOMS's pioneering business model.

Yet TOMS has been attacked for the unintended consequences of its good works and questioned, sometimes harshly, about the effectiveness of its giving model. At the same time, its message—although never its mission—briefly drifted. For years, the business carefully balanced stories about products with stories about giving. But over time, the marketing scales tipped toward lifestyle, which is dangerous when an idea, rather than a shoe, is the heart of your brand. Scaling a for-profit business is hard. So is scaling a philanthropic organization. TOMS's task is doing both, at the same time, and the only way it all works is if one doesn't overshadow the other.[35]

This approach has some vocal critics, including *Shark Tank*'s Kevin O'Leary. "Running a business is hard," the cofounder and chairman of O'Leary Funds told *Inc.*'s Bill Saporito. "You have to be willing to fire your mother. When you are the leader of a business, your responsibility is to the success of the whole organization, not any one individual, including yourself. Successful CEOs know their allegiance must always remain with customers and shareholders, 100 percent of the time."[36]

Yet that opinion ignores trends in both employee and customer sentiment. As Saporito reports:

According to the Deloitte Millennial Survey, 87 percent of millennials believe that a company should have a larger purpose than racking up profits. Consumers in general are also expanding their purchasing criteria. According to a report by the Natural Marketing Institute, those living lifestyles of health and sustainability now represent 22 percent of the consumer base. That's up from 15 percent in 2005. More important, NMI reports a continued "greening" of consumers across the board: The segment of consumers who call themselves "conventional" or "unconcerned" about social responsibility continues to decline. More consumers care, and more care more.[37]

Whatever you decide to do with your company's profits, don't allow those pursuits to distract you from the top priority of earning the money. As Lynn Jurich, cofounder and CEO of solar-panel company Sunrun, told *Inc.*'s Leigh Buchanan, simply talking about being green or ending poverty does little if you're not devoting your energies to making your business reflect your values— and to making your business succeed.

"To massively affect climate change, you need to have mass customer appeal. It's a big, ambitious goal," Jurich says. "A sustainability message alone won't get you there."[38]

Identify what you want your company to stand for—and how, practically, you can achieve its goals beyond expansion and your personal wealth. Which we're about to discuss in the next chapter, as well as how you can continue to personally and financially make a difference to the world.

ENJOYING IT

> One of my early bosses taught me: Invest steadily, a bit out of every paycheck, in up markets and down markets. That way you make it a habit."[1]

SALLIE KRAWCHECK, cofounder and CEO of investment platform Ellevest, author, and former Wall Street executive

> I'm going into my ninth year in the NFL and we are just now moving into our dream house. That's the difference between rich people who keep their money and rich people who lose their money: They both have nice things—houses, cars, the luxury lifestyle—but the ones who are able to keep their money live the luxury lifestyle last, while the ones who lose their money live the luxe life first."[2]

GLOVER QUIN, safety for the Detroit Lions, who lived on about 30 percent of his take-home pay during the first three years of his NFL career

YOUR HARD WORK AND grit and patience have finally paid off: You've taken your business to sustained profitability, or you've sold some or all of it to a deep-pocketed buyer, or you've taken it public. However you got there, it's time to enjoy having money. You've earned it.

Which is something that Sallie Krawcheck knows a lot about, professionally and personally. A widely respected Wall Street analyst in a decidedly #MeToo era (early in her career, male co-workers "put Xerox copies of male nether regions on my desk every day"[3]), Krawcheck rose to become one of the most powerful women in the financial industry. She was CFO at Citigroup, then CEO at Bank of America's Merrill Lynch—and she was fired from both jobs.

Now she's a successful and high-profile entrepreneur, after buying a women's networking company now called Ellevate Network and founding a related digital investing platform for women. She's also a mentor for other female entrepreneurs, including Venus Williams.

Krawcheck regularly advises other professional, high-earning women to be smart with their money, and to pay attention to investing as well as saving, so they can one day enjoy it and use it to pursue their career or personal dreams:

"This entire phase of my career has been about really trying to close the gender money gap," Krawcheck told me in 2017, as we discussed her book on the topic, *Own It: The Power of Women at Work*. "Getting more money to more women is good for women," she continued. "It's good for their families, it's good for the economy, it's good for society, it's good for men—it's just all around good."[4]

If you've reached the point of having more money, you can focus on the fun stuff. But even that requires some advance planning and a lot of expert advice. In this chapter, we'll discuss how to find the right experts to help you manage your money, show you ways to plan for a happy family life and retirement, and provide advice on smart spending splurges—such as "Don't plan a big vacation until the ink is fully dry on the deal to sell your company."

Udi Baron, an Israeli immigrant who moved to Denver to be closer to his wife's family, was running a bakery and restaurant there when someone convinced him to try selling gluten-free bread. Within five years, Baron went from skepticism to running a company that became Udi's Gluten Free, with $125 million in 2012 sales.

That year the company had half of the market for gluten-free bread, and Baron and his partners decided it was time to sell, he told *Inc.*'s Una Morera:

> I'm not a gambler. I'm a paranoid person. And not very brave. When the company was valued at around $100 million, my partners and I all came to the conclusion to sell, to limit our risk. There was always the darkness—the ambiguity— between the time to sell and being too greedy. I still didn't believe the numbers. But we sold for $125 million.

My wife and I had planned to go to the Amazon for two weeks before the deal closed. Our attorneys were horrified. They said, absolutely do not leave until everything is done. So I stayed. On July 3, 2012, I was all alone in my house, waiting for the money to transfer.

When I got the message from my bank, I didn't know how to grasp it. What does it mean to have tens of millions of dollars? What does it feel like to have no worries about money? I went to the supermarket to see if I could understand. I said to myself, "I'm not going to look at the prices. I'm just going to buy everything I want to buy."

From the outside, it might look like, that's what you did? You went to the supermarket and you went shopping? It was the Fourth of July weekend. Everyone was out of town. I had nobody to share it with.

It sounds so weird. But that's how I celebrated.[5]

However you want to celebrate your company's success, you'll need some expert help at this stage, as we previously may have mentioned once or twice in this book.

FIND THE RIGHT EXPERT

Let's be realistic: A lot of the situations you'll face as a business owner will require information beyond what's presented in this book. Those answers will depend on your specific business and personal situation. We've already urged you to hire a professional accountant and a lawyer; now it's time to encourage you to hire a financial advisor, too. *Inc.*'s Alina Tugend has some guidance for how to go about it:

First, some definitions of what can be overwhelming jargon: *Financial advisor* and *financial planner* are generic terms, often used interchangeably. But *certified financial planner* (CFP) refers to someone who has passed exams on topics like taxes and retirement planning and is required to adhere to an ethical code. Meanwhile, a *registered investment advisor* (RIA) describes someone (or a firm) regulated by government securities agencies who gives advice about stocks, bonds, and mutual funds. Many such consultants are both RIAs and CFPs.

Second, the most important word you need to know when looking for financial help is *fiduciary*. That means the person you hire must put your interests before her own, instead of recommending investments that might increase her fees at your expense.

"Keep the word *fiduciary* in mind with anyone you talk to," says Doug Bellfy of Synergy Financial Planning, based in South Glastonbury, Connecticut. "Ask any potential advisor: 'Will you operate under fiduciary duty 100 percent of the time?' That one question cuts through a lot of this complexity."[6]

Barbara Roper, director of investor protection at the Consumer Federation of America, suggests asking an advisor you're thinking of hiring to sign a fiduciary oath. (You can find an example on the National Association of Personal Financial Advisors website.)

She also recommends hiring a "fee-only" advisor—meaning you'll pay the advisor by the hour, by the project, or by a percentage of the assets under management—rather than hiring a "fee-based" advisor, who can also earn commissions from third parties by selling you specific products. Hourly rates for financial advisors tend to run between $150 and $400, depending on an advisor's experience and where you live.

One of the first things you may want to ask your financial advisor for help with is securing your financial future.

PLANNING FOR YOUR RETIREMENT

❝❝ I want entrepreneurs to know that the odds that their company will become a huge success—enough to meet all their financial needs through retirement—are against them. So, it's important to put something aside on a regular basis."[7]

———

JEFFREY LEVINE of Alkon & Levine, a Newton, Massachusetts, accounting firm specializing in small business

Sorry for the cold-water reminder, but planning for your retirement is important long before your business makes you a fortune. In the early days, before you have (m)any employees, you should still be saving money for the future. Even if you're running a solo business and the only retirement planning you have to think about is your own, set aside time to think about how you're going to save for the future.

Time for a little alphabet soup: The most common retirement plan options for business owners are *individual retirement accounts* (IRAs), *solo 401(k)s*, and *simplified employee pensions* (SEPs). As *Inc.*'s Alina Tugend explains, answering the following questions will help guide your decision making. Which plan makes the most sense for you depends on:

→ Do you have employees?

→ What's your tax rate?

→ How old are you?

→ How much can you afford to save each year, and what are each plan's limits?

→ Will you need to withdraw money from the plan before you retire?

Let's walk through your basic options. Note that most of the choices below allow you higher contribution limits if you're at least fifty years old.

→ An *individual retirement account* is the quick and easy option; you can open one with a few clicks and ten minutes at a computer. You'll only be able to contribute $5,500 a year, however. A *regular IRA* will allow you to deduct any contributions from your taxes, but will require you to pay taxes once you start withdrawing those contributions. A *Roth IRA* is the opposite: Your contributions are from after-tax dollars, but withdrawals are not taxed. As Tugend reports, "This is the best option if you're young or don't make much money, because you're in a lower tax bracket and don't need the deductions you get with regular IRAs, says Mari Adam, a certified financial planner and president of Adam Financial Associates in Boca Raton, Florida."

→ A *simplified employee pension (SEP)* is a good option if you want to put away more money. As Tugend reports, "It's popular among business owners with no employees, and the self-employed who want to save more. You may contribute as much as 25 percent of your net earnings," up to $55,000 in 2018.

→ A *solo 401(k)* is another good option if you have no employees (or if you and your spouse are the only two employees). This plan allows you to stash the same percentage of earnings as the SEP and to defer up to $18,500 of your salary annually.

→ A *"simple" IRA*, (for "savings incentive match plan for employees"), as we discussed in Chapter 7, will allow you to cover your employees as well as yourself. Tugend explains, "For small businesses with up to one hundred workers, a simple IRA is usually free and easier to administer than a traditional 401(k). You and employees can each put away $12,500 of your salaries; you usually have to match up to 3 percent of your employees' compensation."[8]

After identifying your initial retirement plan options, you should inquire with your financial advisor about a couple of other topics, including other investment possibilities and your optimal pay structure.

SET UP OTHER INVESTMENTS

You may want to save for other life expenses before retirement, such as property, travel, or your children's college funds. In general, as you pursue other investments, be conservative, look into startup tax privileges, and invest outside of your industry, Allan Roth of Wealth Logic, an investment-advisory firm in Colorado Springs, Colorado, told *Inc.*'s Scott Leibs. Also, don't fall "for the old misconception that your company is the only investment you will ever need," Leibs advises.[9]

For college expenses: If you have kids, look into a 529 plan, which allows you to save money toward education expenses and withdraw the earnings tax-free. "Almost all financial advisors suggest opening a 529, but they differ on how much they recommend putting away," *Inc.*'s Alina Tugend reports:

> For example, don't stop contributing to your retirement when you open a 529, says Bob Morrison, a financial planner with Downing Street Wealth Management. And pay attention to any changes in your kid's college plans. "I don't like to lock a client into a 529 plan if the student does not go to college or does not need all the funds," Morrison says. He suggests putting one-third of your savings into a 529, and splitting the other two-thirds between vehicles like a Roth IRA and a brokerage account. You can withdraw contributions from the latter two without penalty, whether it's needed for college or something else.[10]

TAKE ANOTHER LOOK AT YOUR PAY

This is decidedly advanced-level tax strategy, but you may wish to look into whether you can take some earnings from your business as dividends rather than salary.

Because of the way Social Security benefits are calculated, you could increase your retirement income if you can switch some of your pay to dividends—as long as you have a legitimate reason to do so. According to *Inc.*'s Kathy Kristof, some reasons could include if you can attribute part of your business profits to your employment of other people, or from investments in machinery or other equipment.[11] Consult your accountant before making this switch.

After you've created a plan to ensure your financial future, you might be in a position to indulge in a celebratory reward.

GO AHEAD. SPLURGE A LITTLE.

Buy a car, or a beach house, or a family trip to Disney World. Your hard work has paid off. Enjoy your success and share it with the friends and loved ones who supported you along the way.

Just do so mindfully and carefully. Harold Pollack, the Helen Ross Professor of Social Service Administration at the University of Chicago and coauthor, with *Inc.* "Spread the Wealth" columnist Helaine Olen, of *The Index Card: Why Personal Finance Doesn't Have to Be Complicated*, recently shared some wise advice for founders who have sold their companies, turned wildly profitable, or otherwise experienced a financial windfall:

> If you're patient and lucky and work hard at your business, one day you may find yourself facing the ultimate privileged problem: What do you do with all this money?
>
> It's a question I've been asked frequently . . . from people lucky enough to have become millionaires—but who struggle to manage the dilemmas that accompany visible success, including requests for financial help from friends and relatives, and offers of investment opportunities.[12]

Some of what Pollack advises includes the following:

- → **Continue to live below your means,** and thoughtfully save and invest along with your splurges. Don't rack up new debt to finance those splurges.

- → **Create a reasonable budget to help your loved ones.** Once people in your life know that you're wealthy, you may receive many requests for help, with worthy causes and not, from close friends and family to acquaintances. Set up a specific account for these requests, and stick to its limits.

- → **Don't make any big financial decisions on your own.** You can afford to hire the professionals now—please do so!

- → **Give generously to charitable causes,** but vet where your money is going. Start with Charity Navigator, Give-Well, or Effective Altruism.

PHILANTHROPY AND MAKING A DIFFERENCE

It can be daunting to read headlines about, say, Facebook founder Mark Zuckerberg and his wife, physician Priscilla Chan, setting up a foundation to "cure all disease." (It can seem unrealistic, too.) But many entrepreneurs who've made fortunes from their businesses have decided to be more practical and targeted about their philanthropic causes and goals, which we encourage for you as well.

For example, BlackLine founder and CEO Therese Tucker now runs a company with a market capitalization of around $3 billion.

Despite having sold a majority stake in it to a private-equity firm, and then having subsequently taken it public, Tucker retains an 11 percent stake in the company she started with only her own savings and retirement accounts. By mid-2018, Tucker was worth more than $300 million on paper.[13]

Tucker splurged a bit after her company's IPO—on a Tesla, a purchase she does *not* recommend. ("This is supposed to be the amazing car of the future," she told me, "and the technology was not as advanced as my three-year-old Dodge Durango's." She returned the car, and successfully sued the dealership when it tried to keep her deposit.)[14]

But she also started looking for ways to fund causes that are close to her heart. Tucker's husband is a chaplain at a Los Angeles–area hospital, where he sees many of the area's 58,000 homeless people when they are brought in for treatment. He also witnesses how they lose most personal items in the process.

"The first thing that happens is [the hospital] basically cuts off their clothing and throws it away," Tucker says. As a result, "homeless people will typically not go into the hospital until they're really, really sick." It's not unusual for someone to be forced to check out in a hospital gown or in clothing scrounged from the lost-and-found bins, Tucker says: "It's very demoralizing."[15]

In 2017, Tucker spent several months trying to figure out how she could use her fortune—and work with experienced local nonprofits—to help clothe Los Angeles's homeless population. BlackLine started working with the nonprofit organization Shelter Partnership to distribute 180,000 sweatshirts, pants, underwear, and other clothing items, which were supplied to hospitals, shelters, veterans' agencies, and other organizations.

When I spoke to her about the project in June and then in December of 2017, Tucker was frank about the huge logistical challenges of the effort: "I'm not sure that we've figured out the distribution piece yet, so I'm not sure that it's getting to the right people—and frankly I'm not sure that it's the right stuff yet," she said. "It's an ongoing experiment."

But it's an experiment that's important to her, and that she's spending both her time and her money to solve—while also working with groups that have more expertise.

Your philanthropy doesn't have to be entirely money based either. As stated in Chapter 6, many entrepreneurs set up their businesses from the start to have a charitable component, or organize regular volunteer days for their entire workforce. As *Inc.*'s Liz Welch writes:

Increasingly, business leaders don't think about charities in terms of writing checks but as causes that can unite employees, customers, and communities—and make people feel good about helping in a variety of ways. Blake Mycoskie, founder and "Chief Shoe Giver" of TOMS, started out by donating one pair of shoes to a child in need for every pair purchased. Since 2006, TOMS has supplied more than ten million shoes to impoverished children, and it has taken the same concept to its eyewear line. "Having a purpose behind our products creates a passionate, engaged, and loyal customer base," Mycoskie says. "Our customers are our biggest evangelists—they spread our story far beyond what any traditional marketing would."

For other companies, the focus isn't on far and wide so much as on near and dear. Marty Tuzman, president and CEO of Jenkintown Building Services, a Philadelphia-based exterior building maintenance company with 90 employees, donates the company's services to local causes. "Some of my guys dressed up like Spider-Man and visited the local children's hospital," he says. "We recently did free window cleaning for a homeless shelter after they told us how great it would be to brighten the environment for women who are in some pretty dark places. One of my employees got choked up—he couldn't believe that he was in a position of giving."[16]

Still, Welch cautions, don't do it for the tax write-off—your time won't make any difference to your deductions—and pick a charitable focus that you can stick to, that you have a plan for, and that will help with employee engagement.[17]

SUPPORT OTHER STARTUPS AND ENTREPRENEURS

Once you've made your fortune, another way you can consider giving back is by reinvesting in fellow entrepreneurs. Remember those early chapters about how hard it is for some founders, like women and people of color, to get early funding or make connections? Consider becoming a mentor or angel investor to other startup founders, especially those who might encounter more obstacles when launching their businesses.

Ted Zoller, a Senior Fellow at the Ewing Marion Kauffman Foundation and director of the Center for Entrepreneurial

Studies at the Kenan-Flagler Business School at the University of North Carolina Chapel Hill, has some specific advice for how to approach helping other startups:

→ **Coach.** As an ex-business owner, you know markets, customers, and how to avoid most mistakes (you've made just about all of them). Make connections with companies that interest you and become an informal advisor. Incubators need experienced mentors as well.

→ **Teach.** Entrepreneurial programs have exploded—even at community colleges. Thus, business schools are looking for instructors with small-business experience. Nothing helps the "cycle" more than an influx of rookies. My class at the University of North Carolina, "Launching the Venture," has produced more than one hundred real companies over the past ten years.

→ **Invest.** For ventures you believe in, lead a capital round, form a syndicate, or introduce young founders to your contacts. In the Research Triangle, for instance, about 60 percent of the serial entrepreneurs and investors know one another; in Silicon Valley, the figure is much higher—almost 100 percent. That's a great network for young companies to tap. Join an angel group, or become a limited partner with an established venture fund in the early-stage market and help the firm do due diligence on the rising stars.

→ **Network.** Sponsor events to build the business network. Or just lend your expertise. Does building an entrepreneurial ecosystem really work? Well, I can tell you this from my research: Among "technology-intensive" regions, dealmaker-rich areas, such as the Valley and Boston, always perform better than other metropolitan areas.

The lesson for experienced entrepreneurs? Sell out. But for the sake of your community, keep buying in.[18]

Richelieu Dennis, cofounder and CEO of beauty company Sundial Brands, started the company with his mother and his former college roommate in a Queens apartment in 1991, after he and his family fled Liberia's civil war. Over decades, Dennis built the business from a vendor of soaps on Harlem streets to a conglomerate making SheaMoisture, Madam C. J. Walker, and other hair and beauty products geared toward black customers.

When Dennis sold Sundial to Unilever in 2017, he immediately started using the profits to reinvest in communities that mattered to him. He bought *Essence* magazine from *Time*,[19] and started the $100 million New Voices Fund, which will invest in businesses started by women of color. He hopes the fund will help create fifteen black female millionaires, Dennis told the *Wall Street Journal* in 2018. He's also mentoring fifty women of color, hoping to pass on some of the expertise that helped his business succeed: "We built this business on a micro-level, community by community. That's how it needs to happen," he told the *Journal*.[20]

Philanthropy, paying it forward, an indulgence or two, and retirement investments are just a few ways startup founders enjoy their hard-earned money. However, as previously mentioned, sometimes entrepreneurs feel the urge to reenter the fray of launching another startup.

START ANOTHER BUSINESS

❝ Doing a startup is a choice you have made, so enjoy it and recognize that it can be fun—even though you will have ups and downs. It doesn't really get easier; the challenges just change with time and scale."[21]

—

ALEXANDRA WILKIS WILSON, cofounder of Gilt, Glamsquad, and Fitz

Elon Musk, Jack Dorsey, Sandy Lerner, Toni Ko—these are just a few of the many, many serial entrepreneurs who either start multiple companies simultaneously, or use their fortune from one business to start another (and another, and another).

Entrepreneurship is hard to shake once you've gotten the bug. And starting a second or third business may be easier, now that you know some of the dangers and many of the questions. That will certainly be true if you're starting a business in the same industry—though many entrepreneurs choose to look far afield for new ventures.

Cisco cofounder Sandy Lerner went from big tech to cosmetics (Urban Decay) to, at present, organic farming and food stores (Ayrshire Farm and Gentle Harvest).

Lerner says that what motivates her to start new businesses is outrage: "With Urban Decay, I was outraged that the large cosmetics companies were putting most women in a no-win box—it's not about pink, or about looking like Christie Brinkley. And now, factory farming is a disgrace that appalls me," she says. "But you have to separate outrage from tantrum—and if you want to have a business, you have to have a real product that fills a real need."[22]

If you've found that real product again, or identified a new real need, we hope this book can continue to be a resource for all of the new questions you'll face while building another business. Turn back to the beginning, and good luck!

CONCLUSION

WE HATE TO ADMIT it, but this book probably won't answer every money question you'll have during your business's lifetime. Even if it does, we can't guarantee that it will prevent you from cash-flow worries, payroll shortfalls, or sleepless nights spent worrying about your finances.

What we can promise you is that you are not alone. Every startup founder, successful or not, has struggled with at least some of these questions. The answers they found—or failed to find—have helped inform *Inc.*'s editorial mission for the past four decades and will continue to do so.

And we can refer you back to the Venus Williams quote that opened this book. The only guarantee we can make is that you will make financial mistakes. Fortunately, you're in good company. What will put you among the champions is how you learn from the mistakes you make—and how your business grows stronger from them.

>>>> **SOURCES**

Introduction

1. https://www.inc.com/jeff-haden/how-venus-williams-quietly-
   became-a-successful-entrepreneur-and-why-she-cant-go-
   .html
2. https://www.inc.com/jeff-haden/how-venus-williams-quietly-
   became-a-successful-entrepreneur-and-why-she-cant-go-
   .html

Chapter 1

1. https://www.inc.com/magazine/201706/anna-hensel/
   entrepreneurs-smartest-money-advice.html
2. https://www.kauffman.org/what-we-do/research/kauffman-
   firm-survey-series/the-use-of-credit-card-debt-by-new-firms
3. https://www.inc.com/magazine/201502/leigh-buchanan/bert-
   jacobs-life-is-good-bootstrapping.html
4. https://www.inc.com/magazine/201502/leigh-buchanan/bert-
   jacobs-life-is-good-bootstrapping.html
5. https://www.inc.com/magazine/201604/maria-aspan/stripe-
   online-payments-patrick-john-collison.html
6. https://www.inc.com/magazine/201604/maria-aspan/stripe-
   online-payments-patrick-john-collison.html
7. (*Inc.*, Sept. 2014, page 58)

8. https://www.inc.com/magazine/201605/maria-aspan/baked-by-melissa-ben-ishay.html

9. https://www.inc.com/jason-albanese/how-to-scale-a-business-not-all-business-models-are-created-equal.html

10. https://www.inc.com/magazine/201602/kalee-thompson/where-to-find-good-freelancers.html

11. https://www.inc.com/emily-canal/best-small-cities-for-starting-a-business.html and https://wallethub.com/edu/best-small-cities-to-start-a-business/20180/#main-findings

12. https://www.inc.com/magazine/201602/victoria-finkle/buffer-startup-spending-analysis.html

13. https://www.inc.com/magazine/201412/burt-helm/airbnb-company-of-the-year-2014.html

14. https://www.inc.com/magazine/201412/burt-helm/airbnb-company-of-the-year-2014.html

15. https://www.nytimes.com/2017/03/09/technology/airbnb-1-billion-funding.html

16. https://www.inc.com/magazine/201709/inc-staff/2017-inc5000-ceo-survey-how-founders-launch.html

17. https://www.inc.com/magazine/201706/anna-hensel/entrepreneurs-smartest-money-advice.html

18. https://www.inc.com/magazine/201709/inc-staff/2017-inc5000-ceo-survey-how-founders-launch.html

19. https://www.bls.gov/bdm/us_age_naics_00_table7.txt

20. https://www.inc.com/jeremy-quittner/learnvest-sells-it-self-to-northwestern-mutual.html

21. https://www.inc.com/magazine/201703/kimberly-weisul/inside-job-innovation.html

22. https://www.inc.com/magazine/201405/alexa-von-tobel/need-for-freedom-fund-savings-living-expenses.html

23. https://www.inc.com/magazine/201504/christine-lagorio/bobby-flay-how-i-did-it-cooking-with-gas.html

24. https://www.inc.com/magazine/201804/emily-canal/daymond-john-shark-tank-goals-rise-grind.html

25. https://www.inc.com/magazine/201709/zoe-henry/2017-inc5000-daymond-john-interview.html
26. https://www.inc.com/magazine/201804/emily-canal/daymond-john-shark-tank-goals-rise-grind.html

Chapter 2

1. https://www.inc.com/magazine/201706/anna-hensel/entrepreneurs-smartest-money-advice.html
2. https://www.fedsmallbusiness.org/medialibrary/fedsmallbusiness/files/2018/sbcs-employer-firms-report.pdf
3. https://www.inc.com/magazine/201605/victoria-finkle/startup-budget-cash-flow.html
4. https://www.inc.com/profile/leota
5. https://www.inc.com/magazine/201706/anna-hensel/entrepreneurs-smartest-money-advice.html
6. https://www.inc.com/jeff-haden/how-to-write-a-great-business-plan-key-concepts.html
7. https://www.inc.com/magazine/201706/alix-stuart/legal-entity-type.html
8. https://www.inc.com/zoe-henry/new-tax-law-startups-re-structure-c-corp.html
9. https://www.marketwatch.com/story/should-your-business-be-a-c-corporation-or-pass-through-entity-what-makes-sense-under-the-new-tax-law-2018-07-02
10. https://www.marketwatch.com/story/should-your-business-be-a-c-corporation-or-pass-through-entity-what-makes-sense-under-the-new-tax-law-2018-07-02
11. https://www.marketwatch.com/story/should-your-business-be-a-c-corporation-or-pass-through-entity-what-makes-sense-under-the-new-tax-law-2018-07-02
12. https://www.sba.gov/business-guide/plan-your-business/write-your-business-plan
13. https://articles.bplans.com/a-standard-business-plan-outline/

14. https://www.score.org/business-plan-resources
15. https://www.inc.com/jeff-haden/how-to-write-a-great-business-plan-financial-analysis.html
16. https://www.inc.com/guides/business-plan-financial-section.html
17. https://www.inc.com/guides/business-plan-financial-section.html
18. https://www.inc.com/jeff-haden/how-to-write-a-great-business-plan-financial-analysis.html
19. https://timberry.com/business-plan-expert/
20. https://www.inc.com/magazine/201802/leigh-buchanan-sheila-marikar/first-90-days-startup-launch-guide.html
21. https://www.inc.com/magazine/201710/lindsay-blakely/sweet-green-supply-chain.html
22. https://www.inc.com/magazine/201411/liz-welch/how-i-did-it-matt-maloney-of-grubhub-and-seamless.html
23. https://www.inc.com/magazine/201409/tom-foster/inc.500-companies-who-bootrapped-their-way-to-success.html
24. https://www.inc.com/magazine/201505/leigh-buchanan/the-vanishing-startups-in-decline.htm
25. https://www.inc.com/magazine/201707/lindsay-blakely/how-i-did-it-michael-dubin-dollar-shave-club.html
26. https://www.inc.com/magazine/201706/kimberly-weisul/swell-water-bottle-design-awards-2017.html
27. https://www.inc.com/magazine/201503/tom-foster/the-king-of-kombucha.html
28. (page 58, Sept. 2014)
29. https://www.inc.com/magazine/201706/anna-hensel/entrepreneurs-smartest-money-advice.html
30. https://www.inc.com/magazine/201706/anna-hensel/entrepreneurs-smartest-money-advice.html
31. https://www.inc.com/brenda-barbosa/how-being-nice-to-people-made-bobbi-brown-millions.html

32. https://www.inc.com/brenda-barbosa/how-being-nice-to-people-made-bobbi-brown-millions.html

33. https://www.inc.com/brenda-barbosa/how-being-nice-to-people-made-bobbi-brown-millions.html

34. https://www.inc.com/brenda-barbosa/how-being-nice-to-people-made-bobbi-brown-millions.html

35. https://www.inc.com/magazine/201710/maria-aspan/black-line-therese-tucker.html

36. https://www.inc.com/magazine/201706/maria-aspan/state-of-small-business-lending-infographic.html

37. https://www.fedsmallbusiness.org/medialibrary/fedsmall business/files/2018/sbcs-employer-firms-report.pdf

38. https://www.inc.com/magazine/201605/helaine-olen/how-to-get-a-bank-loan.html

39. https://www.inc.com/ami-kassar/size-matters-sba-some-misperceptions-about-its-loans.html

40. https://www.cnbc.com/2017/05/26/mark-cuban-dont-use-credit-cards.html

41. https://www.inc.com/magazine/201806/harold-pollack/index-card-windfall-financial-advice.html

42. https://www.inc.com/elle-kaplan/want-to-be-a-billionaire-steve-jobs-and-mark-cuban-say-to-do-this.html

43. https://www.inc.com/magazine/201706/anna-hensel/entrepreneurs-smartest-money-advice.html

44. https://www.inc.com/magazine/201802/burt-helm/halo-top-healthy-ice-cream.html

45. http://nsba.biz/wp-content/uploads/2018/02/Year-End-Economic-Report-2017.pdf

46. https://www.inc.com/jared-hecht/what-you-need-to-know-about-financing-your-business-with-a-credit-card.html

47. https://www.fedsmallbusiness.org/medialibrary/fedsmall business/files/2018/sbcs-employer-firms-report.pdf

48. https://www.inc.com/magazine/201605/victoria-finkle/startup-budget-cash-flow.html

49. https://www.inc.com/magazine/201603/jon-fine/food52-amanda-hesser.html

50. https://www.inc.com/magazine/201507/jennifer-alsever/join-the-right-crowd.html

51. https://www.inc.com/kimberly-weisul/five-lessons-from-the-manufacturing-trenches.html

52. https://www.inc.com/magazine/201804/victoria-finkle-kathy-kristof/equity-crowdfunding.html

53. https://www.inc.com/magazine/201804/victoria-finkle-kathy-kristof/equity-crowdfunding.html

54. https://www.inc.com/magazine/201409/darren-dahl/inc.500-ross-edwards-build-group-launching-under-pressure-works.html

55. https://www.inc.com/magazine/201502/liz-welch/new-york-citys-chocolate-king.html

56. https://www.inc.com/magazine/201502/liz-welch/new-york-citys-chocolate-king.html

57. https://www.inc.com/magazine/201802/mailchimp-company-of-the-year-2017.html

58. https://www.inc.com/magazine/201802/mailchimp-company-of-the-year-2017.html
Chapter 3

1. https://www.inc.com/magazine/201411/jon-fine/how-to-work-with-your-spouse-without-killing-each-other.html

2. https://www.inc.com/magazine/201604/maria-aspan/stripe-online-payments-patrick-john-collison.html

3. https://www.inc.com/magazine/201808/jane-porter/how-i-did-it-moe-momtazi-maysara-wines.html

4. Interview, June 12, 2018, Dublin, MoneyConf

5. https://www.inc.com/magazine/201802/leigh-buchanan-sheila-marikar/first-90-days-startup-launch-guide.html

6. https://www.inc.com/magazine/201802/leigh-buchanan-sheila-marikar/first-90-days-startup-launch-guide.html

7. https://www.inc.com/magazine201406/jessica-bruder/how-to-balance-company-and-marriage.html

8. https://www.inc.com/magazine201406/jessica-bruder/how-to-balance-company-and-marriage.html

9. https://www.inc.com/magazine201406/jessica-bruder/how-to-balance-company-and-marriage.html

10. https://www.inc.com/magazine201406/jessica-bruder/divorce-tips-for-entrepreneurs.html

11. https://www.inc.com/magazine/201705/maria-aspan/flying-high.html

12. https://www.inc.com/magazine/201705/maria-aspan/flying-high.html

13. https://www.inc.com/anna-hensel/daymond-john-smartest-money-advice.html

14. https://www.inc.com/guides/201106/how-to-get-drama-free-funding-from-parents.html

15. https://www.inc.com/guides/201106/how-to-get-drama-free-funding-from-parents.html

16. https://www.inc.com/magazine/201802/leigh-buchanan-sheila-marikar/first-90-days-startup-launch-guide.html

17. https://www.inc.com/minda-zetlin/4-smart-ways-to-protect-yourself-when-family-members-invest-in-your-startup.html

18. https://www.inc.com/magazine/201505/david-whitford/john-mackey-whole-foods-icons-of-entrepreneurship.html

19. https://www.inc.com/magazine/201605/maria-aspan/baked-by-melissa-ben-ishay.html

20. https://www.inc.com/magazine/201702/sheila-marikar/better-halves.html

21. https://www.inc.com/magazine/201702/sheila-marikar/better-halves.html

22. https://www.inc.com/magazine/201806/maria-aspan/wawa-convenience-store-pennsylvania.html

23. https://www.inc.com/magazine/201806/maria-aspan/wawa-convenience-store-pennsylvania.html

24. https://www.inc.com/magazine/201806/maria-aspan/wawa-convenience-store-pennsylvania.html

Chapter 4

1. https://www.inc.com/magazine/201706/anna-hensel/entrepreneurs-smartest-money-advice.html

2. https://www.inc.com/magazine/201510/scott-gerber/sandy-lerner-exit-interview.html

3. https://www.inc.com/magazine/201407/robin-schatz/how-to-choose-and-get-accepted-to-an-accelrator.html

4. https://www.inc.com/zoe-henry/angela-benton-how-to-lean-into-fear.html

5. https://www.inc.com/zoe-henry/angela-benton-how-to-lean-into-fear.html

6. https://www.inc.com/magazine/201407/robin-schatz/how-to-choose-and-get-accepted-to-an-accelrator.html

7. http://www.seedrankings.com/

8. https://www.inc.com/kimberly-weisul/the-best-startup-accelerators-in-the-us.html

9. http://www.seedrankings.com/#about

10. https://www.inc.com/managing/articles/200806/rajamaran.html

11. https://www.inc.com/magazine/201505/graham-winfrey/lessons-from-the-private-equity-playbook.html

12. https://www.inc.com/magazine/201606/alix-stuart/corporate-venture-funding.html

13. https://www.inc.com/magazine/201606/alix-stuart/corporate-venture-funding.html

14. https://www.inc.com/magazine/201507/jennifer-alsever/join-the-right-crowd.html

15. https://www.inc.com/magazine/201802/leigh-buchanan-sheila-marikar/first-90-days-startup-launch-guide.html

16. https://www.inc.com/magazine/201804/maria-aspan/christina-tosi-milk-bar-momofuku-bakery.html

17. https://www.inc.com/magazine/201303/how-i-got-started/sandy-lerner.html

18. https://www.washingtonpost.com/lifestyle/food/cisco-cofounder-sandy-lerners-next-big-idea-redefining-road-food/2016/10/28/e8772d48-9b01-11e6-9980-50913d68eacb_story.html?utm_term=.3d172e71341a

19. https://www.inc.com/magazine/201804/kimberly-weisul/bre-pettis-danielle-applestone-makerbot-othermill-3d-printer.html

20. https://www.inc.com/magazine/201804/maria-aspan/christina-tosi-milk-bar-momofuku-bakery.html

21. https://www.inc.com/magazine/201804/maria-aspan/christina-tosi-milk-bar-momofuku-bakery.html

22. https://www.inc.com/magazine/201410/liz-welch/bre-pettis-makerbot-exponential-growth-3d-printer-company.html

23. http://www.nber.org/papers/w22587

24. https://www.inc.com/christine-lagorio/inside-beyonce-investment-in-watermelon-water-wtrmln-wtr.html

25. https://www.inc.com/christine-lagorio/beyonce-knowles-backs-wtrmln-wtr-juice-startup.html

26. https://www.inc.com/magazine/201710/zoe-henry/wanderu-polina-raygorodskaya.html

27. https://www.inc.com/magazine/201710/zoe-henry/wanderu-polina-raygorodskaya.html

28. https://www.inc.com/magazine/201710/zoe-henry/wanderu-polina-raygorodskaya.html

29. Victoria Finkle, "What Do VCs Want?" *Inc.*, October 2017, page 58–59 (not online)

30. https://www.bcg.com/publications/2018/why-women-owned-startups-are-better-bet.aspx

31. https://www.inc.com/magazine/201611/kimberly-weisul/new-face-of-funding.html

32. https://www.inc.com/magazine/201611/kimberly-weisul/new-face-of-funding.html

33. https://www.inc.com/magazine/201611/liz-welch/busting-out-feminine-product-revolution.html

34. https://www.inc.com/magazine/201710/jeff-bercovici/stitch-fix-katrina-lake.html

35. https://www.inc.com/magazine/201505/helaine-olen/how-to-join-the-venture-backed-fraternity.html

36. https://www.inc.com/kimberly-weisul/seven-signs-that-women-entrepreneurs-are-about-to-rake-in-the-dough.html

37. https://www.inc.com/salvador-rodriguez/arlan-hamilton-backstage-capital.html

38. https://work.qz.com/1264481/the-improbable-rise-of-americas-hottest-vc-arlan-hamilton-founder-of-backstage-capital/

39. https://www.inc.com/magazine/201702/diana-ransom/founders-forum-care-dot-com.html

40. https://www.inc.com/kimberly-weisul/how-to-raise-venture-money-female-founder-raised-100-million.html

41. https://www.inc.com/magazine/201412/alicia-robb/how-crowd-wisdom-closes-the-gender-gap.html

42. https://www.inc.com/magazine/201411/lindsay-blakely/how-jessica-alba-proved-her-doubters-were-wrong.html

43. https://www.inc.com/maria-aspan/policygenius-insurance-jennifer-fitzgerald-raising-money.html

44. https://www.inc.com/maria-aspan/policygenius-insurance-jennifer-fitzgerald-raising-money.html

45. https://www.inc.com/maria-aspan/policygenius-insurance-jennifer-fitzgerald-raising-money.html

46. https://www.inc.com/magazine/201307/jessica-bruder/how-to-pitch-a-vc.html

47. https://www.inc.com/magazine/201510/helaine-olen/its-nice-to-be-wanted-but.html

48. "What Do VCs Want?"

49. https://www.inc.com/magazine/201804/annalyn-kurtz/term-sheet-funding.html

50. https://www.inc.com/magazine/201804/maria-aspan/christina-tosi-milk-bar-momofuku-bakery.html

Chapter 5

1. https://www.inc.com/magazine/201407/tom-foster/michael-dell-on-transformating-dell.html

2. https://www.inc.com/magazine/201407/tom-foster/michael-dell-on-transformating-dell.html

3. https://www.inc.com/magazine/201612/will-yakowicz/jeff-lawson-twilio.html

4. https://www.bizbuysell.com/news/Small-Business-Transactions-Reached-Record-Highs-in-2017-up-27-Percent-from-2016-According-to-Bizbuysell-Report

5. https://www.renaissancecapital.com/IPO-Center/Stats/Pricings

6. https://www.ey.com/Publication/vwLUAssets/an-analysis-of-trends-in-the-us-capital-markets/$FILE/ey-an-analysis-of-trends-in-the-us-capital-markets.pdf

7. https://www.inc.com/magazine/201410/david-whitford/inc.-35th-anniversary-aaron-patzer-charles-schwab.html

8. https://www.inc.com/magazine/201703/kimberly-weisul/inside-job-innovation.html

9. https://www.bizbuysell.com/news/Small-Business-Transactions-Reached-Record-Highs-in-2017-up-27-Percent-from-2016-According-to-Bizbuysell-Report

10. https://www.inc.com/30under30/2008/profile/5-patzer.html

11. https://www.inc.com/magazine/201410/david-whitford/inc.-35th-anniversary-aaron-patzer-charles-schwab.html

12. https://www.inc.com/magazine/201410/david-whitford/inc.-35th-anniversary-aaron-patzer-charles-schwab.html

13. https://www.inc.com/magazine/201612/kathy-kristof/leaving-your-partners.html
14. https://www.massmutual.com/~/media/files/business-owner-perspectives-study.pdf
15. https://www.inc.com/magazine/201402/jennifer-alsever/business-for-sale-market-booming.html
16. https://www.inc.com/bob-house/how-small-business-sellers-can-keep-momentum-going-in-2018.html
17. https://www.inc.com/bob-house/6-ways-to-increase-the-value-of-your-business-before-you-sell.html
18. https://www.inc.com/magazine/201505/liz-welch/barbara-corcoran-shark-tank-icons-of-entrepreneurship.html
19. https://www.inc.com/magazine/201707/lindsay-blakely/how-i-did-it-michael-dubin-dollar-shave-club.html
20. https://www.inc.com/magazine/201703/kimberly-weisul/inside-job-innovation.html
21. https://www.inc.com/magazine/201703/kimberly-weisul/inside-job-innovation.html
22. https://www.inc.com/sonya-mann/ikea-taskrabbit-ethnography.html
23. https://www.inc.com/sonya-mann/ikea-taskrabbit-ethnography.html
24. https://www.nytimes.com/2018/07/13/business/stacy-brown-philpot-taskrabbit-corner-office.html
25. https://www.inc.com/magazine/201402/jonathan-sposato/lessons-from-selling-to-google.html
26. https://www.inc.com/magazine/201402/jonathan-sposato/lessons-from-selling-to-google.html
27. https://www.inc.com/magazine/201402/jonathan-sposato/lessons-from-selling-to-google.html
28. https://www.inc.com/magazine/201512/jeff-bercovici/slack-company-of-the-year-2015.html
29. https://www.bloomberg.com/news/articles/2018-08-21/slack-s-valuation-rises-to-7-1-billion

30. https://www.inc.com/magazine/201607/christine-lagorio/toniko-nyx-cosmetics-perverse.html

31. https://www.inc.com/magazine/201806/maria-aspan/ken-moelis-company-investment-bank-ipo.html

32. https://www.inc.com/magazine/201510/tom-foster/do-you-really-want-to-go-public.html

33. https://www.inc.com/jacqueline-kelley/play-the-long-ipo-game.html

34. https://www.renaissancecapital.com/IPO-Center/Stats/Pricings

35. https://www.inc.com/magazine/201604/leigh-buchanan/founders-40-2016-sunrun-lynn-jurich.html

36. https://www.inc.com/magazine/201702/will-yakowicz/zendesk-copenhagen-wall-street.html

37. https://www.inc.com/magazine/201806/maria-aspan/ken-moelis-company-investment-bank-ipo.html

38. https://www.inc.com/magazine/201806/maria-aspan/ken-moelis-company-investment-bank-ipo.html

39. https://www.inc.com/magazine/201604/jeff-bercovici/founders-40-2016-fitbit-eric-friedman-james-park.html

40. https://www.inc.com/magazine/201510/tom-foster/do-you-really-want-to-go-public.html

41. https://www.inc.com/magazine/201705/jacqueline-kelley/founders-10-2017-stock-price-ipo.html

42. https://www.inc.com/magazine/201504/leigh-buchanan/grabbing-a-seat-at-a-much-bigger-table.html

Chapter 6

1. https://www.inc.com/magazine/201509/leigh-buchanan/your-awkward-phase-and-why-you-should-love-it.html

2. https://www.inc.com/leigh-buchanan/jessica-matthews-will-never-run-out-of-energy.html

3. https://www.inc.com/magazine/201112/evernote-2011-company-of-the-year.html

4. https://www.inc.com/magazine/201509/leigh-buchanan/your-awkward-phase-and-why-you-should-love-it.html
5. https://www.cbinsights.com/research/venture-capital-funnel-2/
6. https://www.cbinsights.com/research/venture-capital-funnel-2/
7. Interview, July 2018
8. https://www.inc.com/kevin-j-ryan/pymetrics-replacing-resumes-with-brain-games.html
9. Interview, July 2018
10. https://www.inc.com/magazine/201303/robin-d-schatz/how-we-got-funded-betterment.html
11. https://www.prnewswire.com/news-releases/betterment-raises-additional-70m-with-the-goal-of-becoming-the-most-loved-financial-services-company-of-a-generation-300491943.html
12. https://www.inc.com/zoe-henry/inc-uncensored-jonathan-neman-keach-hagey-stacey-abrams.html
13. https://www.inc.com/zoe-henry/inc-uncensored-jonathan-neman-keach-hagey-stacey-abrams.html
14. https://www.inc.com/elliot-bohm/debt-funding-vs-venture-capital-what-mix-is-right-for-your-business.html
15. https://www.inc.com/magazine/201710/maria-aspan/blackline-therese-tucker.html
16. https://www.inc.com/magazine/201605/leigh-buchanan/toms-founder-blake-mycoskie-social-entrepreneurship.html
17. https://www.inc.com/magazine/201605/leigh-buchanan/toms-founder-blake-mycoskie-social-entrepreneurship.html
18. https://www.inc.com/magazine/201706/anna-hensel/entrepreneurs-smartest-money-advice.html
19. https://www.inc.com/magazine/201602/helaine-olen/startup-burn-rates-spend-money-to-make-money.html
20. https://www.inc.com/magazine/201809/kimberly-weisul/ellen-pao-project-include-metoo-women.html
21. https://www.inc.com/magazine/201509/kate-rockwood/2015-inc5000-a-pivot-a-therapist-and-a-revival.html
22. Interview, July 2018

23. https://www.inc.com/magazine/201402/jill-hamburg-coplan/
    cash-flow-squeeze-growth-companies.html
24. https://www.inc.com/magazine/201402/jill-hamburg-coplan/
    cash-flow-squeeze-growth-companies.html
25. https://www.directcapital.com/blog/business-insights/finance-
    lending/top-cash-flow-management-tools/
26. https://www.inc.com/magazine/201602/victoria-finkle/buffer-
    startup-spending-analysis.html
27. https://www.inc.com/magazine/201610/alina-tugend/
    chargebacks.html
28. https://www.inc.com/magazine/201703/victoria-finkle/
    tipsheet-cybersecurity.html
29. https://www.eater.com/2018/2/15/16974980/cashless-
    restaurants-credit-card-only-legal-problem-discriminatory
30. https://www.inc.com/zoe-henry/inc-uncensored-jonathan-
    neman-keach-hagey-stacey-abrams.html
31. https://www.inc.com/magazine/201605/victoria-finkle/startup-
    budget-cash-flow.html (in infographic)
32. https://www.inc.com/magazine/201808/helaine-olen/how-to-
    find-a-better-accountant.html
33. https://www.inc.com/magazine/201808/helaine-olen/how-to-
    find-a-better-accountant.html
34. https://www.inc.com/magazine/201706/kate-rockwood/
    business-insurance-tips.html
35. https://www.inc.com/magazine/201706/kate-rockwood/
    business-insurance-tips.html
36. https://www.inc.com/magazine/201602/deirdre-van-dyk/do-
    you-really-need-a-lawyer.html
37. https://www.inc.com/magazine/201602/deirdre-van-dyk/do-
    you-really-need-a-lawyer.html
38. https://www.inc.com/magazine/201802/annalyn-kurtz/hiring-
    foreign-workers-immigration.html
39. https://www.inc.com/magazine/201605/victoria-finkle/startup-
    budget-cash-flow.html

40. https://www.inc.com/magazine/201706/anna-hensel/entrepreneurs-smartest-money-advice.html

41. https://www.inc.com/guides/2010/10/how-to-budget-and-manage-inventory-for-2011.html

42. https://www.inc.com/magazine/201511/graham-winfrey/preparing-for-the-pop.html

43. https://www.inc.com/magazine/201511/victoria-finkle/choose-your-own-manufacturing-adventure.html

44. https://www.inc.com/magazine/201511/victoria-finkle/choose-your-own-manufacturing-adventure.html

45. https://www.inc.com/donna-fenn/2016-30-under-30-uncharted-play.html

46. https://www.inc.com/donna-fenn/2016-30-under-30-uncharted-play.html

47. https://www.inc.com/magazine/201505/scott-gerber/exit-interview-ayah-bdeir.html

48. https://www.inc.com/magazine/201702/jeff-haden-bill-saporito/venus-williams-cover-story.html

49. https://www.inc.com/jeff-haden/how-venus-williams-quietly-became-a-successful-entrepreneur-and-why-she-cant-go-.html

50. https://www.inc.com/jeff-haden/how-venus-williams-quietly-became-a-successful-entrepreneur-and-why-she-cant-go-.html

51. https://www.inc.com/magazine/201706/anna-hensel/entrepreneurs-smartest-money-advice.html

52. https://www.inc.com/magazine/201602/victoria-finkle/buffer-startup-spending-analysis.html

53. https://www.inc.com/magazine/201602/victoria-finkle/buffer-startup-spending-analysis.html

54. https://www.inc.com/magazine/201505/graham-winfrey/neil-blumenthal-icons-of-entrepreneurship.html

55. https://www.inc.com/christine-lagorio/turning-point-parachute-retail-decision.html

56. https://www.inc.com/magazine/201808/maria-aspan/how-i-did-it-philip-krim-casper.html

57. https://www.inc.com/magazine/201602/tom-foster/kevin-plank-under-armour-spending-1-billion-to-beat-nike.html

58. https://www.inc.com/bill-green/thinking-about-expanding-your-business-heres-why-you-should-consider-acquiring-an-other-company.html

59. https://www.inc.com/bill-green/thinking-about-expanding-your-business-heres-why-you-should-consider-acquiring another-company.html

60. https://www.inc.com/bill-green/thinking-about-expanding-your-business-heres-why-you-should-consider-acquiring-another-company.html

61. https://www.inc.com/magazine/201602/tom-foster/kevin-plank-under-armour-spending-1-billion-to-beat-nike.html

62. https://www.inc.com/magazine/201705/zoe-henry/will-amazon-buy-you.html

63. https://www.inc.com/magazine/201407/adam-bluestein/how-to-maintain-company-culture-after-an-acquisition.html

64. https://www.inc.com/magazine/201702/kate-rockwood/tip-sheet-social-media-influencers.html

65. Simona Covel, *Marketing Your Startup: The Inc. Guide to Getting Customers, Gaining Traction, and Growing ther Business* (New York, AMACOM, 2018), 31–32.

66. https://www.inc.com/magazine/201502/liz-welch/new-york-citys-chocolate-king.html

67. https://www.inc.com/magazine/201710/victoria-finkle/setting-your-own-salary.html

68. https://www.inc.com/magazine/201504/david-whitford/gamergate-why-would-anyone-want-to-kill-brianna-wu.html

Chapter 7

1. https://www.inc.com/magazine/201707/maria-aspan/how-i-did-it-jack-ma-alibaba.html

2. https://www.inc.com/magazine/201602/victoria-finkle/buffer-startup-spending-analysis.html

3. https://www.inc.com/magazine/201809/kimberly-weisul/ellen-pao-project-include-metoo-women.html

4. https://www.inc.com/magazine/201707/maria-aspan/how-i-did-it-jack-ma-alibaba.html

5. https://www.inc.com/magazine/201804/leigh-buchanan/lean-startup-job-creation.html

6. https://www.inc.com/magazine/201806/christine-lagorio/chobani-yogurt-hamdi-ulukaya-hiring-refugees.html

7. https://www.inc.com/magazine/201806/christine-lagorio/chobani-yogurt-hamdi-ulukaya-hiring-refugees.html

8. https://www.inc.com/magazine/201806/jeff-bercovici/asana-best-workplaces-2018.html

9. https://www.inc.com/magazine/201606/maria-aspan/best-workplaces-2016-commonbond.html

10. https://www.inc.com/magazine/201806/tom-foster/lord-green-best-workplaces-2018.html

11. https://www.inc.com/magazine/201606/inc-staff/best-workplaces-2016.html

12. https://www.inc.com/magazine/201806/helaine-olen/gender-pay-gap-women-equitable-wage.html

13. https://www.inc.com/magazine/201605/etelka-lehoczky/salary-transparency-company-strategy.html

14. https://www.inc.com/magazine/201607/jill-krasny/sharing-equity-workers.html

15. https://www.inc.com/magazine/201607/jill-krasny/sharing-equity-workers.html

16. https://www.inc.com/magazine/201710/helaine-olen/professional-employer-organizations.html

17. https://www.inc.com/magazine/201710/helaine-olen/professional-employer-organizations.html

18. https://www.inc.com/magazine/201605/kathy-kristof/best-employee-retirement-plan.html

19. https://www.inc.com/magazine/201510/helaine-olen/help-your-employees-hit-their-targets.html

20. https://www.inc.com/magazine/201510/helaine-olen/help-your-employees-hit-their-targets.html

21. https://www.inc.com/magazine/201611/kathy-kristoff/retirement-save-more-pay-less.html

22. https://www.inc.com/magazine/201510/helaine-olen/help-your-employees-hit-their-targets.html

23. https://www.inc.com/bartie-scott/paid-family-medical-sick-leave-is-good-for-business.html

24. http://www.ncsl.org/research/labor-and-employment/paid-sick-leave.aspx

25. http://www.ncsl.org/research/labor-and-employment/state-family-and-medical-leave-laws.aspx

26. https://www.inc.com/magazine/201603/saki-knafo/best-parental-leave-policy-options.html

27. https://www.inc.com/magazine/201606/minda-zetlin/unlimited-vacation-benefits.html

28. https://www.inc.com/magazine/201511/diana-ransom/creative-perks.html

29. https://www.inc.com/magazine/201702/helaine-olen/company-retreats.html

30. https://www.inc.com/magazine/201804/minda-zetlin/sexual-harassment-workplace-policy-metoo.html

31. https://www.inc.com/magazine/201412/paul-keegan/the-new-rules-of-engagement.html

32. https://www.inc.com/magazine/201505/graham-winfrey/neil-blumenthal-icons-of-entrepreneurship.html

33. https://www.inc.com/magazine/201605/leigh-buchanan/toms-founder-blake-mycoskie-social-entrepreneurship.html

34. https://www.inc.com/magazine/201605/leigh-buchanan/toms-founder-blake-mycoskie-social-entrepreneurship.html

35. https://www.inc.com/magazine/201605/leigh-buchanan/toms-founder-blake-mycoskie-social-entrepreneurship.html

36. https://www.inc.com/magazine/201603/bill-saporito/shark-tank-kevin-oleary-be-evil.html

37. https://www.inc.com/magazine/201603/bill-saporito/shark-tank-kevin-oleary-be-evil.html

38. https://www.inc.com/magazine/201604/leigh-buchanan/founders-40-2016-sunrun-lynn-jurich.html

Chapter 8

1. https://www.inc.com/magazine/201706/anna-hensel/entrepreneurs-smartest-money-advice.html

2. https://www.inc.com/magazine/201706/anna-hensel/entrepreneurs-smartest-money-advice.html

3. https://www.inc.com/maria-aspan/sallie-krawcheck-qanda.html

4. https://www.inc.com/maria-aspan/sallie-krawcheck-qanda.html

5. https://www.inc.com/magazine/201808/una-morera/how-i-did-it-udi-baron-udi-s-breads.html

6. https://www.inc.com/magazine/201610/alina-tugend/finanicial-adviser-what-to-know-first.html

7. https://www.inc.com/magazine/201402/scott-leibs/investing-for-entrepreneurs.html

8. https://www.inc.com/magazine/201603/alina-tugend/best-retirement-tools-entrepreneurs.html

9. https://www.inc.com/magazine/201402/scott-leibs/investing-for-entrepreneurs.html

10. https://www.inc.com/magazine/201605/alina-tugend/college-savings-planning.html

11. https://www.inc.com/magazine/201711/kathy-kristof/social-security-retirement-income.html

12. https://www.inc.com/jessica-stillman/can-all-the-financial-advice-you-need-fit-on-an-index-card.html

13. https://www.forbes.com/profile/therese-tucker/#623bf90e 219a
14. https://www.inc.com/magazine/201710/maria-aspan/ blackline-therese-tucker.html
15. https://www.inc.com/maria-aspan/blackline-homeless.html
16. https://www.inc.com/magazine/201405/liz-welch/ entrepreneurs-pursue-philanthropy-in-new-ways.html
17. https://www.inc.com/magazine/201405/liz-welch/how-startups-can-be-smart-about-giving-to-charities.html
18. https://www.inc.com/magazine/201405/ted-zoller/what-small-business-owners-do-after-cashing-out-matters.html
19. https://www.inc.com/sonia-thompson/essence-just-took-lead-in-serving-women-of-color-heres-why-it-matters-now-more-than-ever.html
20. https://www.wsj.com/articles/a-day-in-the-life-of-sundial-brands-cofounder-richelieu-dennis-1525270384
21. https://www.inc.com/project-entrepreneur/this-female-founder-serial-entrepreneur-solves-problems-for-women-heres-why-that-makes-sense.html
22. https://www.inc.com/magazine/201510/scott-gerber/sandy-lerner-exit-interview.html

>>>> **INDEX**